To the Boathouse

To the Boathouse

a memoir

MARY ANN CAWS

The University of Alabama Press Tuscaloosa

Library of Congress Cataloging-in-Publication Data

Caws, Mary Ann.
    To the boathouse : a memoir / Mary Ann Caws.
        p. cm.
    ISBN 0-8173-1425-3 (cloth : alk. paper)
    1. Caws, Mary Ann. 2. Caws, Mary Ann—Childhood and
youth. 3. Caws, Mary Ann—Homes and haunts—North Carolina. 4. English teachers—United States—Biography. 5. French
teachers—United States—Biography. 6. North Carolina—Social
life and customs. 7. Critics—United States—Biography. I. Title.
    PE64.C39A3 2004
    809—dc22

                                        2004001805

The recipe for Chef's Cathedral Pudding is reprinted courtesy of
National Cathedral School, Washington, D.C. Quotations by
Eudora Welty are from "Place in Fiction," *Stories, Essays, and
Memoir* (New York: Library of America, 1998), 793. The memory
of "downhome" in chapter 1 is from Susie Mee, *Downhome:
An Anthology of Southern Women Writers* (Orlando: Harcourt
Brace, 1995); and the quotations by Walker Percy are from *Sign-
posts in a Strange Land* (New York: Farrar Straus Giroux, 1991).
The quotation by Mark Doty in chapter 7 is from *Still Life with
Oysters and Lemon* (Boston: Beacon Press, 2001).

For my family and friends

It is by knowing where you stand that you grow able to judge where you are. . . . It is the sense of place going with us still that is the ball of golden thread to carry us there and back and in every sense of the word to bring us home.

—Eudora Welty, "Place in Fiction"

Contents

Preface

It was raining last night, incessantly, beating down on the New York pavements. When I picked up the mail, there was the annual newsletter of the Sweetbriar Junior Year in France, with the group photograph of my year's students on the ship going over. I saved it for last, in a kind of nostalgia that went well with the rain. There were all my classmates, all smiling, looking very 1950s. I couldn't find myself in the group: I was just not there with the others. That's what it often felt like growing up and then afterward, not being wherever I was. I would never have expected to see so clear a picture of my absence.

In grade school, in my North Carolina town, I always seemed to be joining my class long after school had started, and my parents were always taking me out before things had finished. The reasons must have made sense then, even if I can't recall them now. All I remember is the feeling of something inappropriate. When I was supposed to have a piano recital, someone made a recording of my playing instead. It felt like never being anywhere at all.

I never asked any questions.

There's a long tradition of daughters not talking, not telling, not speaking up—not just in the South, of course, but our personal and family mythologies feel so strong there. This tale was to be called an autofiction, as half-true as are all memoirs. In any case it's a meditation and a wondering.

It's taken me a while to do that, to wonder why I didn't seem to have a voice for so long, to ask or to talk about things. Why I didn't seem to have any real place to start out from. Yet there was a place that I could probably see if I tried hard enough. I wanted it to be home, and I suppose it was. Or perhaps it becomes so now when I find my voice to tell about it, from this other home, so different. I've wanted my voice and my place to coincide. And I think they may, at last.

Acknowledgments

OVER THE YEARS DURING WHICH I was writing this memoir, many friends have been generous in their reading and listening. Some of them appear in these pages explicitly; all were important to it. My gratitude to each of them: Susan Adler, Ann Aslan, Gina Barreca, Boyce Bennett, Clive Blackmore, Hilary and Jonathan Caws-Elwitt, Matthew Rorison Caws, Peter Caws, Linda Collins, Patrick Cullen, Katherine Dalsimer, Alice Dark, Morris Dickstein, Diana Festa, Carolyn Heilbrun, Gerhard Joseph, Arnold Krupat, Arlyne Landesman, Nancy K. Miller, Ned Perrin, Christopher Prendergast, Peg Rorison, Grace Schulman, Hedda Sterne, Janet and Malcolm Swan, Patricia Terry, Baylis Thomas, Frederic Tuten, and Sarah Bird Wright.

My agents, Katherine Fausset and Gloria Loomis, offered their encouragement and their counsel, as did the staff of The University of Alabama Press. During a crucial stage of the thinking out of the text, I was privileged to have the idyllic surroundings of Bellagio, thanks to the Rockefeller Foundation. More recently, I have had the encouragement of the Women Writing Women's Lives seminar, at which I read several passages from this story. For all this, I am thankful.

To the Boathouse

One

Southern Vines

WHAT WAS IT LIKE IN the South, my northern friends ask. How to explain it? I could, for a start, quote to them one southern woman's memory of "downhome" as an example of the landscape and mindscape: "It's made up of particular smells: honeysuckle and nasturtium, spring arriving early and staying late, wet woods, pine fire, cigar smoke and tobacco juice, the inside of mountain cabins, hot irons on starched dresses, dusty dirt roads, a jarful of lightning bugs, . . . and tastes: spring water, a Dr. Pepper drunk outside a filling station on a summer afternoon, greens, butter beans." But my memories are very different.

Much of what I felt about the South I knew when I was young carried with it a special, valuable kind of loneliness: the mimosa scent everywhere, and what we called the banana shrub, the rituals of society and church, the heavy shade trees, dripping with silvery gray moss, the sun setting over the mournful swamps with the cypress stumps lurking in them. The magnolias for climbing in and hiding in, for smelling the enormous creamy blossoms with their yellow center; the pine forests with the tall trunks standing so prickly against the sky, their gobbets of sap you could feel, protruding from the trunks; the bay trees with the leaves you could crumple and smell, like some place far away; those clumps of bamboo and cedar with hollow middles, rising so high that you could sit alone and not be reached. I never wanted to be reached.

I understood all too well what Walker Percy meant by "the placeness of the South" becoming too suffocating for some writers. That was not the reason for my leaving. Yet that placeness seems to nourish everything I remember now.

SWINGING OUT

Our town looked, so long ago, like a lot of towns in North Carolina, I expect. It was quiet and you could usually make time for what you wanted to do. I remember most, growing up in an outlying part called Oleander, how my sister, Peg, and I would make time for going down to the river. It wasn't much of a river, really, sort of a creek, with insects flitting back and forth. But we called it "the river."

Bright green wings I remember, and the water a muddy brown. And vines growing up along the trees and winding down again in a dark tangle. You would take hold of the one that seemed the right length for that particular day, swing on it way out over the water, and drop down on the other side. Right before you would grab it, you would get a terror in your knees, and worse right before dropping. I never got over it. What Peg felt, I don't know. I couldn't seem to ask her about it. Right now, I can feel that swoop in the pit of my stomach.

The trees crowded close together by the creek to make a perfect place for secrets, away from the light, twisting and murky. Sometimes there were several of us over by the vines, but I liked best being there just with Peg. We had something special between us: hard to say what. Mother used to ask me about it; Father never did. When we'd had enough swinging, we'd go behind the vines, and smoke a bit of rabbit tobacco in the circle of the bamboo grove, hidden away. That was where Peg told me about life. I surely wasn't going to ask our parents about anything. It wasn't actually a family in which you wanted to ask a lot. Whatever kept us quiet, it had gotten all tangled up, worse than the vines. You couldn't see the bottom or where it started, or how to untangle it.

When we were growing up, we lived in a largish house of Anglo-Norman design. Our father had been a pilot in the war, and was afterward connected with Security National, a small southern bank that was later absorbed by Wachovia, then by North Carolina National. Since Mother's father had been invited over from America to work in the cotton business in Bremen owned by the Sprunts, lifelong friends of the family in our town, Mother was brought up abroad. Upon her return, she mixed up her languages, as well as her metaphors, with a good deal of charm. "That's the way the anvil swings," she would say. It swung in my mind for years, and still does upon occasion.

After returning to America during the war, mother was placed in National Cathedral School in Washington, D.C. Subsequently, instead of going to college, she went to Charles Rann Kennedy's acting school somewhere up North, and it had made a big impression on her: melodrama was a part of her makeup. If she never did learn anything practical, such as spelling, refilling a ballpoint pen, or adding a row of figures, she could write a letter with all the downstrokes heavy and the upstrokes delicate, as she had in Europe. She could name the days of the week in several languages, and you would think it was poetry. What she had was a kind of elegance. She was much admired, in spite of never getting the hang of southern rhythm.

Mother's great-grandfather General Clayton had been the president of the University of Alabama in 1912. They had all grown up near there, in Eufaula. Others in the family had been senators and lawyers. Grandmother, the one I adored and wanted to be just like, was called to Washington, to be the hostess for Senator Pugh, her uncle I think. About our father's family, we knew less, except that his mother, Ama, was said never to have looked in a mirror. It was claimed that some aunt died in her rocking chair rather than admit she had no food. We found all this impressive and strange.

Everything was very neat around Mother and Father. It seemed the exact opposite of the intertwining tangle of those vines I loved so much. In the off-white bedroom with the massive French furniture Mother had "antiqued" a dull green, they had twin closets. Father's cordovan loafers from Clark's in England, several pairs, shiny and fragrant with the Kiwi polish he used every night, were lined up at the bottom of his closet. The sweet smell of the polish lingered in the room. The heel of each right shoe was built up three-fourths of an inch to compensate for his shorter leg. His gray suits hung next to his tux and tails, his white shirts were perfectly folded in the sliding drawers of the antiqued dresser, with the cuff links for his French cuffs stored in a little round horn box on top of the dresser.

Mother's dresses all draped loosely from their hangers, arranged by color. At the bottom of her closet were drawers for scarves and jewelry boxes. Three long necklaces, amber, jade, and lapis lazuli—you had to be as tall as she was to wear them—hung over the little earphone by her dresser, put in long ago to communicate with "the servants" of whom there was now just one, Nunny. Mother would never have thought of talking with Nunny on that phone; she would rather go downstairs and have a chat. Nunny would certainly prefer that also: I never knew why the little phone remained there.

Mother wore flat shoes, so that she would not tower over Father, which she did in any case. His short stature had saved him once, she told us, when an enemy bullet had left a deep mark in the top of his pilot's helmet. He had been shot down several times, but never talked about it. Or much of anything else that seemed important to me.

Father never spoke to us about his past, although we would have liked him to. We were not supposed to ask about that or indeed anything at all. We weren't told that, I think, but we just knew.

> *In a typical dinner table scene Peg is asking about Father's vote in the recent elections: the world comes to a halt. His hands shaking, his voice also, he announces she has no right to ask that, or in fact anything. Neither of us has enough knowledge to have any opinions. Fine with me: I hate having opinions. So I get in less trouble than Peg, but feel guilty over that.*

> Would you say something to your daughter, dearest? She's asking questions again!

> *At Father's outburst, Peg bursts into tears and flees the room. I stare at my plate and cross my fingers so it won't happen to me. If I don't say anything, maybe he won't yell at me.*

> *Peg rushes upstairs sobbing, trying not to make any noise. Next time, she says to me later, next time I'll take a deep breath to remember not to ask anything ever.*

Or then sometimes Father and Peg would start arguing, who knows about what. It could be politics or God, or something else. Father would raise his voice slightly, his hands trembling. Peg would look scared, and then suddenly it would all fall apart. Mother and I would take the dishes to the kitchen and leave them together. You couldn't do any good anyway when voices started rising. Sometimes the atmosphere would clear, sometimes not.

If Mother had been in the kitchen, could she see what had happened after-ward by Peg's eyes the way I could? Often, you couldn't guess what Mother was thinking and I didn't want to ask. I guess it was not asking Father that made me hesitate to ask anyone else anything.

Generally Mother was perceptive, easily pleased, interested in everything, and somewhat different from other people, as if she were holding something in reserve. Or not knowing how to share it. When the rain was pouring down warm on the slate roof, she might sometimes try to explain to us how things were and had been, over the gingerbread and syrupy sauce she felt appropriate to the rain. The way she and her three brothers had been brought up in Bremen haunted her all her life. She would tell us tales of how her German governess loved to frighten her by saying there was a rabbit in the toilet. If she hit a wrong note, the piano teacher would rap her knuckles until they bled. The sewing teacher would rip out her knitting over and over: "Amerikanische," she would hiss, and drop a box of pins on the floor for Mother to pick up. Her three brothers would scalp her dolls. It was not a good time for her.

When World War I broke out, the family made their way back through England, leaving Mother's brother Max to be schooled. They returned to Wilmington, to a large and rambling house downtown, across from Grand-mother's friend Miss Nellie. When Mother was in drama school as a budding actress, she had shown great talent. But she ended up in southern society, in which her slightly foreign manners and her natural warmth mingled well with her beauty. Mother rode horses and dressed with great dramatic flair. Five men proposed to her, but she chose the one who was her best friend. I liked that story a lot. Some day, I used to think, when I had a best friend who was of the other sex, I'd like to marry him.

In the stories Mother used to love to tell us, you could hear a dim kind of melancholy: inherited from Germany, I thought. All her tales were tinged with it. Little Mary Rose was always getting lost in the forest; a small boy was always being swept away by the king of death—"the Erlkönig," Mother would exclaim—and Paula Modersohn-Becker, the friend of Rilke, was always dying in childbirth. Grandmother had known Paula and her hus-band, Otto Modersohn, when she had been invited to paint in the Worp-swede school, near Bremen. Paula Modersohn's depressing and intimately foggy colors my mother loved in art and life.

Mother remained haunted by her time growing up in Germany as a foreigner. She would recite with fevered intensity:

Ich weiss nicht was soll es bedeuten
Das ich so traurig bin . . .

translating for me: "I don't know why I feel so sad. . . . "

I associated this poem with a large and florid painting of the Lorelei that hung above our stairs. She had nothing whatsoever to do with sadness, this frontally posed, bare-breasted female. She was on the contrary so joyously exposed that Mother would take her off the wall if visitors were coming. Their discomfiture at such an extraordinary sight she could scarcely imagine. As for the firemen, for example, too bad: I think they would have loved it, as I did. I always took a look to get up my courage before sliding down the curving brass banister.

Mother's style was effortless and visible everywhere, even in mundane things. For picnics, she could make the thin slices of cucumber rest just against the edges of the bread with its crust cut off, whereas my thickish chunks would protrude from the sides or tear unsightly holes in the bread. She would take us to sit on a sand dune by the ocean at Wrightsville Beach—not far from Oleander—or in some forest nearby, and tell us fables. They seemed less sad when we were on picnics than the bedtime tales she would tell when sitting on the edge of our beds, before we fell asleep. Among the picnic stories, I especially liked the one about the jam spoon that kept filling back up. It was the opposite of poor little Mary Rose and the doomed son. But Mother liked the heavy forest-sad ones better.

Mother said often she had had a happy life, but it looked to me like a constant taking care of others, once she was married. Her parents had given the young couple the house we grew up in, in Oleander, on Live Oak Parkway: everything was named after trees or flowers. For years, "Big Sister," our father's aunt, lived with us, bedridden and sitting straight up, her lace peignoir and her perfectly arranged hair beribboned in pale blue, in a room at the top of the stairs, where the door was never shut. She needed to know every single thing that went on: she delighted in disapproving of many. She wanted to see who was going up and down, and for what reason.

Mother took care also of her brother-in-law, delicately Leslie-Howard handsome and shell-shocked from the war. He had been in the RAF, and afterward, incapacitated and kindly, he lived over our garage. Mother, who was never known to complain, had also to take care of her husband, my father, limping from the war and with several ribs missing—as well as Grandmother, and both of us, to say nothing of the church poor. And the memories in the graveyard.

My sister Peg I always adored. She could get me into my pajamas quicker than anyone, knew exactly what I wanted to read, and read it with me. Not at me, but with me. A faded brownish photograph shows us kneeling side by side. We are supposed to be praying, and indeed Peg's eyes are closed and her face is serious. My eyes are wide open and I seem to be waiting for something to happen. She was sincere at praying, as at everything, and I was curious and suspicious. I didn't want to miss out.

Peg was older and went away to school, to National Cathedral as Mother had, and as I did later. I loved it when she came home on vacations. Her being at home would change everything, just like the sun shining. We would get up early and go on "expeditions," where we could talk things out.

> *Peg coming in as a ghost during pajama parties, blowing in a Coke bottle with a satisfactory spooky sound. Rum and nuts and macaroons and ginger Mother would heap with a large spoon over the ice cream, it all feeling like plenty. Like the jam spoon filling itself back up.*

Behind our house, a gigantic magnolia tree bent low down, so heavy in white fragrance that I couldn't concentrate when I read in the branches. They were just wide enough to perch on and those leaves thick enough to hide in. I would go there to worry. My relations to the magnolia tree and to the God I prayed to in that tree and in the few other places where I felt safe, were very close for a while, and intertwined. I always loved, from the beginning of Sunday school, the small dramatics of praying aloud, in the rich cadences of the King James version of the Bible.

Still little, I once lost a silver spoon I had been digging with. As punishment, I had to choose between switching and spanking. If you chose switching, you had to choose your own switch. The thin ones hurt the worst, because they cut right in. The point was to choose a sturdy one while you kept looking frail so you wouldn't be switched hard. If you chose spanking, it was never with a bare hand, so you could figure out which side of the hairbrush would hit you: it was worse on the bristly side.

Apparently, God helped me find the spoon, when I sent up an urgent request. But a few weeks later, he let me down. I taped a prickly question on my wall, written very large in capital letters. I stuck it there and went for a walk, sure the answer would be there when I came back, taking long enough for it to get thought through:

Dear God, are there fairies?

He never answered, so I assumed he didn't know either.

> *It is a late October Sunday. I am sitting in the magnolia tree with my cocker spaniel puppy, Carbon Tetrachloride, on my lap. He runs out in front of the red car that kills him. It is my fault for not caring enough about God, I know it. When I run into the house to tell my mother, she says: "That's all right, darling. We'll get you another dog." I yell at her that she doesn't understand, it or me or anything, and go up to pack my knapsack to leave forever.*
>
> *Later, I go down to supper. No one mentions the event. Mother probably didn't even hear me.*

Wisteria vines climbed up the side of the pale pink brick parish house where we practiced in the Saint James choir. When I yawned all the way through every service, Scottie the organist said that was good: it meant you opened your mouth wide and really sang. Wearing those heavy black robes with the starched white collars to sing in church made up for the slightly boring ceremony, of which I only liked the hymns. I had always wanted to be a nun and wear a habit, but there were not many Anglican orders and none nearby. I liked the Lenten services best, at five in the afternoon, mournful and solemn. Always I counted the mistakes in the sermons, read the words of all the hymns, and all the articles of the faith I was supposed to have, and all the rules of the rituals, in the back of the prayer book. But God hadn't taken the time to answer me about the fairies.

On Sundays, we were always late for church. When I had to go up the aisle (I was always wearing the wrong thing, wasn't I?) to put the tasteless wafer on my tongue and take a sip of the communion wine, even that little sip would make me dizzy. Weaving my way back to my seat, I would try not to let on how lightheaded I had become from the wine, or to show how I was concerned with the way the hot-air vent would blow my pleated skirt up and out.

Mother would whisper:

Darling, you do look so gloomy!

I guess I did. Who could be at ease in church? My face would keep going wrong, so once safely back in the pew, I would hide it against the wood of the pew in front of ours, as if in prayer. I was always concerned not to let on to my family how weak my faith was. When we said the creed, we had to stand straight up and not hold on to anything—I wobbled a bit, and was careful not to say aloud the parts I didn't believe in, mumbling my way through those. I had asked our family friend, sweet-faced Bishop Thomas Wright, what to do about saying the creed if you didn't believe in much of it: he said God wouldn't be insulted, just go on and don't hurt your family. That sounded right to me.

I liked it best when Bishop Wright would intone the Nunc Dimittis, my favorite prayer, in closing, so quietly you couldn't really hear all the words. But I knew them and loved them:

Lord now lettest thou thy servant depart in peace,
According to thy word . . .

The sound of peace would stay in my mind for a while. I was especially glad that to know that it "passeth understanding." Maybe I could find it later.

I'm so glad you're here

I found myself saying to Bishop Wright afterward, but of course that was where he was supposed to be. Where was I supposed to be?

After coming home from church, it was my duty to empty the pint of vanilla ice cream from its cardboard package into the metal ice tray, taking out the cubes for Father's drink. I'd lick the spoon when I'd put the ice cream in. It made a smooth coating.

The person Peg and I were closest to was Nunny, with us since Peg was born. Under the white napkin she wore around her hair, telling us, with her enormous smile, it was an Ethiopian turban, she could wiggle her ears and wink. She'd cook things she'd call a "layover to catch meddlers." She'd make a sticky sugar sauce to harden on ice cream or tiny "dollar" pancakes, when she wasn't cooking collards or field peas and okra. Those green and brown vegetables were all slimy, but you could get them down with a big enough slice of the crumbly yellow cornbread I loved, hot from her oven. Nunny liked to serve us a dish of cool clabber for dessert, letting the rich milk poured from the bottle with the cream on top sit out on the porch all night until it turned solid. I would douse it with sugar until it crunched. And sprinkle nutmeg over it.

We all spent a lot of time in the graveyard. At Easter, we would take pink and white flowers; at Christmas, wreaths and holly, to all the family graves. I loved some of them, like the grave of little Charlie, with a tiny lamb by his stone. And I loved going by Nunny's on the way to the graveyard, because she made stocking dolls with glass eyes that looked right at you. Mother would always take us away in a hurry, as she did from everywhere. I guess she never liked to linger. "Your mother still lunning?" asked the Chinese laundry man after her death. I hope she is.

> I am sitting in the kitchen with Nunny at the marble-top table. She has made some nut cookies and put six aside, three for Peg and three for me. I have eaten Peg's as well as mine: they were very good. "How could you do that?" Nunny asks. I don't know. I sit there wondering.

No one could have protected us from our father's occasional anger. That he cared for us so much made his usual silence more of a strain. He must have been doing his best. Maybe that's what he always did. I think that now. He would take Peg and me, with one friend each, to the circus. Once I remember shouting in joy from the Ferris wheel, and then shutting up, embarrassed. No one seemed to notice.

Other times, we would all go out at night to shoot at candles propped against a tree trunk, or at noontime, at matchbook covers tossed in the air, on the radiant beach. We loved to watch the seagulls overhead, because we had read Paul Gallico's *Snow Goose*. I like to think we read it aloud to each other, but perhaps not. Like listening to the Longines music hour together. Or to the opera with Mother, over tea.

The best times were always on trips—easier than being at home. I was never sure why. At the beginning of every trip:

Off for a good time,

Father would say, and off we went for just that. Even when I used to throw up around every river or mountain bend, or Peg got one of her headaches. He was always in a good mood away.

When Peg or I went off to school in Washington, he would fill our pockets with change he measured out as "chicken feed," although it wasn't that to us, or to him. We were of Scottish ancestry and bore all the traits of it. Old MacDonald, of the Isle of Skye, Father would say, and get out his clan book. The Coast Line Railroad used to have its headquarters in Wilmington, so the train would start out from there. Just before I would get on the steps, Father would hand me a pack of postcards addressed to himself. At first, they were to Mother and him, and later, just to him; I never thought to wonder why. Years later I kept finding little piles of these, when it was too late to send them. The postage rate had changed a dozen times, and Father was not anywhere to be reached.

As the train pulled out, Nunny would stand near the tracks and wave us off. Long after there was no more Coast Line, the station would still be there, the white marble halls echoing with footsteps from the past.

SCHOOL IN WILMINGTON

School was always a strange place to go to or come home from. When I was little, I won a writing prize at Forest Hills grammar school near Oleander—everything was named after flowers or trees there, like Live Oak Parkway, where we lived. I ran all the way home to tell Mother. "Fishing pond's closed," she said. By which I suppose she meant I shouldn't fish for compliments: I didn't realize I was, just wanted to tell her. So I didn't talk about school any more at home. There were lots of things not to talk about.

Later I went downtown to New Hanover High, for two years. Miss Walsh, the high school English teacher, had to pin her beige skirt to her beige blouse since she was all one shape up and down. She kept goats at home, in a little shed at the back. I kept asking to be driven by her house hoping to see the little shed, and maybe just one goat. I never did.

In Miss Bradshaw's Latin class, the horrible Dudley sat behind me; once he undid my bra right through my blouse in the back, when I wouldn't show him my exam paper and the answers. I spent a good part of my time in school wondering how I could get my arms to look all brown and fashionable like Snookie's. Her real name was Gertrude, but Snookie seemed just fine. No one would dare to fool with her. No one would be looking at her papers on quizzes. What about telling on people, I wondered. Say, on Dudley. I didn't know whom to ask about this one, since Peg was away at school. I didn't feel like asking Father. Mother would have her mind on other things, so that left my best friend, Sarah Bird, who always knew about things.

So what do I do?

When I asked her, we were sitting in Papa Joe's on Market Street near the high school, making our Orange Crushes last, in their dark green bottles. Sarah Bird was wearing her blue green sweater that set off her green eyes behind the horn-rimmed glasses she was trying out. She would always try out things for two or three weeks to be sure they'd work in her system.

She carefully weighed all the possibilities and their outcomes, depending on how they would fit into whatever plan she had in mind. I didn't actually have one of those, but I did grasp that you had to work out things for yourself. I never did say anything to Miss Bradshaw about Dudley. I guess I knew I wouldn't.

Sarah Bird

Sarah Bird had the house next to our cottage at Wrightsville Beach, where we lived all summer. She has always been my closest friend. She is as neat as I am chaotic, as focused as I am distracted. When I would go to Papa Joe's at lunchtime to have a vanilla shake and grilled cheese with tomato, Sarah Bird, who came in from the beach to high school, would take her sandwich from home to read with *War and Peace*, saving her allowance for records of

Beethoven symphonies. Sarah Bird was logical and organized, could put things and people in shape, including herself, and me, her friend. She had Values.

Her family, so different from mine, was informal. I used to envy her, spending as much time at her house at the beach as I could when we lived there in the summers. In her family, whatever she wanted to ask, she could, and she would get the answers. We would sit on her porch and swing our feet out over the rungs of the green rocking chairs. Shelley, her family's cook, made the world's best pecan pie. Her mother would cut up carrot sticks for me. There at her house looking over the body of water we called "the sound," I felt at home, more than at my house.

Her roof sloped invitingly. It was green, and her house was white. Ours, right next to hers, was grayish, its long porches open on the sound, where the rain would beat down in diagonals, and the sun would make a shield of light. Sarah Bird and I would send messages back and forth on a pulley we rigged up between our adjoining houses. We would crawl out her window to lie on her roof, not too near the edge, but scary all the same, right by the metal gutter. We liked to sing mushy songs about bravery and imagine ourselves deeply, tragically, in love:

> Though you walk through the rain, keep your head up high,
> And don't be afraid of the dark. . . .

If our songs weren't about the weather and courage, they were about the ocean and loss:

> Et la mer efface sur le sable . . .
> Les pas des amants désunis.

Ah, wonderful: the ocean was erasing from the sand the steps of those lovers, parted forever. Absolutely, forever, as it had to be. We loved the melancholy of it all. Like the quietness of the beach, mixed with the gray of sky and sea. Never would we want lovers who'd remain: no, their steps would have to be erased. If the ocean didn't do it, we would.

Sometimes we would walk to Station One, the drugstore at the end of the beach, picking up empty bottles on the way, all we could find, until we had enough bottles to turn in for pennies to buy the latest Wonder Woman comics. Sarah Bird liked the way the bullets bounced off her thick iron bracelets, left and right, Zoing!!! Zoing!!! I liked her tiara. She had real spunk, and we both liked that. It took many bottles to buy an issue. Dawn was the best time to gather them from the beach, if my family would let me go out so early.

WRIGHTSVILLE BEACH

We lived in our beach cottage in the summer, in the months we did not have to rent it to others. "It has to stand on its own," Mother would say. We lived there and then we left; I tried never to think of the others who lived there when we didn't. It was managed politely by an agent, Mrs. Hinnant, as I remember. I had a talent for not noticing displeasing things. Maybe that stood me in good stead later, maybe not.

When we lived in our cottage, Peg and I divided up our loyalties and our ways of feeling between the ocean and the sound, over which our long porches with their green wooden floors and white banisters seemed poised. Precariously, because almost every fall, some hurricane with a female name— Ursula, Edna, Ida, and so on—would take off their banisters and the roof of the cottage and mean many repairs. I blamed the hurricanes for our having to rent the cottage out for so many months.

On sunny days, and some overcast ones, we might walk beside the ocean, on the beach we reached by crossing the paved road, with the tar burning our feet. You had to choose between that and the sandspurs beside the road. Peg would take the sandspurs every time. I guess that's about the only thing we didn't agree on. Sarah Bird would alternate.

The beach was long and dull white or a faint yellow if the sun was up, with the water gray or green. We'd walk up and down for ages with no one else around anywhere, making wavy lines with our bare toes that we'd re-trace going back. The tide would roll in faster than we could pull back, spattering over us. The little sand crabs skittered everywhere, over the rivulets in the sand, and around the shell of a skate always lying there.

At twilight the air went gray too, the sea smell rising. You never know, we'd say to each other, one of these times we just might swim over to Shell Island, across the current at the tip of our beach. If we didn't do it, that didn't mean we wouldn't some time soon. Just saving it up, like we did lots of things. Mother was a superb swimmer, in both sound and ocean, and rode the waves better than anyone, in the roughest water. Peg and I would go over to the ocean to see if it was a day when we could brave the undertow or, if it was calm, let the water wash over us. The ocean was always different.

The sound on which our cottage and Sarah Bird's house were built was a miraculous body of water with no currents or waves, only tides that would come noiselessly in and out and change entirely the way things looked and were. Little sandfiddlers with huge claws rushed about on the sand at low tide. In that tide too, you could set bait to catch the scary bluish crabs from the pier, making your way over the wooden slats and peering down to see if any were hanging on. Then you would bring out the long nets and scoop them up, trying not to let them out onto the pier where they would scuttle after you with one large claw raised. In the tin bucket, they would scrabble around and you would try not to listen or look. It was Nunny who would plunge them into the cold water to be slowly heated so they would simply snooze off, as she described it. I hoped that was the way it was.

You could read out on the end of the pier at the wide part, if the sun wasn't too high and nobody was around. Any time, you could walk out and just look at the water, but it was the high tide that was magical. In a sense, the tides ruled our lives there. You never swam in the sound at low tide, and so the announcement: "High Tide!" came as a call to action, always followed by my favorite words in the English language: "How about a swim?"

It was where you would swim if you wanted no interruptions to your thought. You could just meander around with slow strokes or take it more rapidly if you felt like it. Peg would do a snazzy Australian crawl across to the other side in the early morning, over and back in an hour or less. Mother swam in the ocean to ride the waves with her peerless technique, or did the sidestroke in the sound, always at the same pace. Father never swam; he preferred his boat. I loved both bodies of water, like Mother. I liked to dive from our pier right into the water if I was alone at high tide, but if I was with Mother, we would take our time and swim together.

Mother had, I think, always done the sidestroke, and if you did it across from her, with your legs and arms going the opposite way from hers, you could talk with her. We used to do this when I was little, and kept it up. I think those were the times we were closest, without interruptions or social rules. How I loved those easy times, going with the current. Even when we had to struggle against it, we felt together. Maybe especially then. We never talked about it.

You couldn't breathe after lunch in the summer. It was stifling, out and in. Rules were simple in our house: no bare feet at lunch. No talking politics or religion, but we wouldn't have anyway: what did we know? . . . Lunch was fish and hominy grits, runny and grainy when hot, congealing around the butter pat in the middle soon after. The black wooden table gleamed from its polish, the iced-tea spoons clattered in the tall glasses, and my grandmother's still lifes shone from the walls. I loved every one of them, with the ginger jars and the brocade cloths.

The summers of polio epidemics, you couldn't go out, so Sarah Bird and I, and Peg when she was there, played endless games of Go Fish and Monopoly. I liked Marvin Gardens and the little dark green houses, while Sarah Bird liked the blue Park Avenue buildings and the red hotels. We both hated Baltic Avenue in purple.

Every time there was a hurricane warning, Sarah Bird would spend the night in town with me in Oleander, when we had moved back from the beach. Mother would tell us stories about dying children or fairies, and let us drink hot chocolate. At Easter time, Sarah Bird would come in too, and look with me for the little bright jelly beans Mother had hidden in all the corners of the living room and under the cushions. First in Sarah Bird's room, then in mine, in the early morning, Mother would bring in a plate of freshly cut orange sections, and prop us up on our pillow with a book. And would say to each of us—as she always had to Peg, remembering Grandmother, and in just the same bright tone:

Have you used Pears soap this morning, dear?

Our bookcases were full of things German and French and English, and Mother was always full of projects.

Every time, your mother put on a different play for us,

said Sarah Bird years later, when I was trying to remember.

She had the art of making every day special. Remember how she would transform the whole house for a hurricane? Remember how she rented that boat on the other side of town? Remember how she'd read Shakespeare to us, and toast marshmallows with us, remember all those conversations at dinner, those picnics? Remember the Easter eggs she hid, and the tower of the church at five on Easter morning? Every day she offered me a thousand childhoods I never had.

COMING TO CALL

In Oleander, as all over the South, somebody was always coming to call. It went on endlessly. Sometimes the ladies would bring cookies or watermelon pickles in light green squares with lots of syrup. That part I liked, because I would always have a few of them before Nunny or Mother would put them away.

When I'd hear someone coming, I'd look out from the window in my little bathroom above the paving-stone path by the laurel tree. If it was somebody I liked, I'd go down, otherwise not unless I had to. Sometimes Mother asked me to tell stories about school, if I wasn't in the mood to recite one of my mournful poems. I'd make up some outlandish things, but nobody ever questioned me if I smiled at them. I smiled a lot.

Whoever it was, I was supposed to "draw them out." The best way was to ask them some advice or other. Miss Katherine or Miss Jocelyn were likely to stay about an hour and a half, with sherry or coffee in the morning, or with tea and biscuits in the afternoon. They might talk about what they put in the church bazaar to make money for the poor, or about the new minister. I learned to put on an interested face. For the bazaar Mother would make things out of shells, paint trays and little stools to sit on, while the others made cakes and casseroles. Miss Katherine would always buy Miss Jocelyn's things; Miss Jocelyn would buy Miss Katherine's things; and Mother, or Grandmother if she was filling in, would buy both Miss Katherine's and Miss Jocelyn's. Mother's creations would disappear quickly, of which we were all very proud, even Father.

I would look at the light striking the side of Miss Jocelyn's steel-rimmed glasses just fitting over the top of her ear and under her blue hair, and see how her leather shoes shone. If it was raining, she would wear her black shoes. Miss Katherine carried in her pocketbook exactly what Mother did: an emery board and a lace-edged handkerchief. The way the Harvey's Bristol Cream looked, shining golden in the glass decanter, was just like its nutty taste. I would pass around the tiny beaten biscuits set on the napkin crisply folded, with the thin slices of Virginia ham sticking out between the layers, then eat several of them on the way to the kitchen, saving two or three more to have upstairs while I wrote more poems. If it was winter, we would have iced Sally White fruitcake, with angelica and citron in it, but it would fall apart, so it was harder to take upstairs.

Once in a while I would shut myself away upstairs by the window in my room to write my poems, all of them rhyming, desperately sad, and definitely mediocre. Occasionally, Mother would ask me to read a few, and everybody would very politely go "ah." Mother had a group of them printed, under a cover where the title was blue against white: "Leaf-Lined Grey," it said. I couldn't stand the thought of just blue sky: our own was often gray. One poem began:

I picked some flowers today, John,

And I can't remember who John was . . .

PEG

If I can whistle at all, it's because Peg taught me ages ago. We'd go for a long walk out into Piney Woods, near Oleander, where we walked a lot, the two of us. I think it was our favorite walking place, next to the ocean, of course. The resin got all sticky in the sun and exuded that strong smell. The little gobbets of resin would burst if you pushed on them, hot in your hand. We'd end up by lying on our backs to take a little doze, or try to work some things out, or just be quiet, looking up through the spindly trees to the sky. You could smell the sea somewhere not too far off. If it was early enough, the day would have a kind of shimmer on it.

I always thought our whistles went well together, although Peg's sounded more confident. We made a good team that way and others. She would talk to people, I'd size them up without saying much. I never did. I might have wondered at some things; there didn't seem to be too much point in asking about them. Peg knew how to ask, and so she learned a lot more than I did.

The pine trees had tall, knotted trunks. We'd sit against the fattest ones we could find and chew on a piece of sour grass. Or then on that sturdy green kind that you could wet and hold between your thumbs to blow through. It would tremble back and forth in that little space in the middle, making a sharp sound. Peg would start whittling at whatever she could find: she could whittle anything. She would look at some piece of wood and you could see her itching to get to that old army knife Father had given her. She carried it everywhere, bulging out of her pocket, in case we'd come across something, some piece of wood or other. It had to be on the ground already: no way either of us was going to pull something off a tree.

Our favorite place was these woods with the pine needles scrunching under your feet. If I wore my shoes with the little holes in the top ("breathe-easy," they said on the package), I could feel the needles sticking in a little.

The rain is beating down on the azaleas, magenta—the color I most hate—and white. On the slate roofs, on the magnolia trees with their creamy blossoms hanging down around the central cone. On those feathery mimosas smelling pink, on the bay tree by the old wall. I lie down on the sidewalk in my school clothes and let it go all through me. When I arrive home drenched, Mother just smiles.

In our house in Oleander with its casement windows, pitched slate roof, and dark paneling, our favorite radio programs—Hop Harrigan, Terry and the Pirates, the Gray Ghost, the Shadow (Who knows what evil lurks in the hearts of men? The Shadow knows . . .)—are constant visitors. They are realer than we are. But at least we can all listen together. Like playing quadruple solitaire.

FAMILY THINGS

Mother wanted to teach me to sew, although I never saw her doing it except on Saturday afternoons in the winter, listening to the Texaco Opera from the Met. I was impatient, just like the times when Grandmother wanted to teach me to paint. You would think I never wanted to learn anything. Milton

Cross would tell us about *Tosca* or some other opera. He always sounded enthusiastic, in spite of those incurably grim plots. Between stitches, Mother would point out how much better off I'd be not wearing high collars that gave me no neck. She might have been thinking about the no-neck monsters in Tennessee Williams, but never said that. What she did say was Miss Annie Grey Sprunt had said that ladies shouldn't ever wear turtleneck sweaters. And that if you grinned the way I did at times, your cheeks would get very fat. But then she would give me a hug, and I would grin as hard as I could. I was just plain ornery, as Nunny sometimes pointed out.

My other favorite thing to do was to go to Clarendon, Grandmother's old riverside plantation, not far from Wilmington, but on a canal. There, green gray moss hung on all the trees. At night, the alligators snapped along the canal, where my mother and father used to paddle in the early morning hours, looking for bluebells. There were goats about, munching whatever they found, and green lizards sunning themselves. Glass doors led from room to room, and through them Mother's elegant guests had once chased a greased pig, at one of the parties she used to give. The person who pinned down the pig was awarded some prize or other. . . . Mother had planned to write a children's book about life on a plantation—I found her notes on a scrap of paper:

> For children aged 6 to 10 or 12:
> Describe Living on an Old Plantation around 1912. Riding bareback over fields. The house backyard with rules for hitting branches of huge oak trees when playing tennis. "Hound dogs" with corn pones thrown them—Cold clear water from the well. Watermelons—swimming in a pond—snakes occasionally plopping into the water.—Fear of a huge one rolling down the hill after us. Brothers' horses, one wild, my fast but gentle one. Of my grandmothers surprise gift under a basket on the porch—of ghosts down the long driveway—of rabbit & squirrel hunting & possum too—of my mother's church going in Eufaula & in the tiny Clayton church for which my great-grandmother sold cream for buying the organ.

Grandmother had rented Clarendon out to the novelist Inglis Fletcher one year; she was writing *Lusty Winds for Carolina,* in which there was supposed to be something about the Earl of Clarendon. I found it incredibly romantic to have rented something to a novelist, since I'd have liked to be one.

GRANDMOTHER

After she rented it no one talked about the plantation, and it was sold. Grandmother's house in the mountains, that timbered "cottage" in Linville in the Smoky Mountains in western North Carolina, with its bark shingles, forget-me-nots in the surrounding ditches, and greener grass than anywhere, was given to our Savannah family. Peg and I had spent part of our summers there, when the Wrightsville cottage was rented. We would walk in the woods, clamber up the mountains, and look for wild strawberries on the slopes. Grandmother's studio used to be in the back, behind the wall of stone, covered with vines, and just beyond the ditch full of forget-me-nots. It smelled, like her studio at home, of turpentine and linseed oil; here it mixed with the smell of pine.

I loved to look at that angular plaster head she would keep by her, and the changing faces of her models on the stands around the room. She would show me how you could use just a bit of red or cadmium yellow to make the rest of the painting stand out, telling me how Corot used his dot of red among his grays and greens. Among the many colors she used to show me on her palette, I especially loved the names of burnt sienna, umber, and cornelian red. Her face would shine when she painted. I never stopped longing to care about something that much.

> I love it when Grandmother wipes her fingers with turpentine onto her smock. I love the light in her eyes when she starts a new "subject." She has always painted, all her life, and most of all wanted for me to want that too. I wouldn't have had the patience to continue, I tell her.

With her watching, long ago, I did an oil, of magnolias. I could smell them with their thick perfumed blossoms you could bury your nose in. But I got bored with oils and wanted to try something else, so I did a charcoal, a still life, with a plate of royal Doulton china. And then I stopped. I remember saying:

Do you want me to try pastels?

No, said Grandmother, I want you to do what you are doing. She was look-ing at me hard.

I would run my fingers over the angles of the skull she modeled from, and the bust of the mysterious Unknown Woman from the Louvre she always had by her, who looked even sadder than Mother sometimes looked. Often I had to sit for a portrait for hours, sometimes for Grandmother's friends, like Alphaeus Cole, whose father was the more famous Thomas Cole. Some-times I would sit for Grandmother herself, while Mother read to me from the books I chose, always about artists or actresses. Grandmother measured me with her finger held up, smiling from time to time. I would have been like her if I could.

Grandmother spent much of her time making things for other people, to have at home or to take to them when they were sick or were entertaining: cookies, muffins, cakes. She gave me some of her favorite recipes, on paper now yellowed. I haven't tried them, but I can taste them still.

Grandmother's Cheese Soufflé
⅓ pound cheddar cheese
⅓ cup of milk
2 tablespoons bread crumbs
3 eggs, separated

Grate the cheese, and add the warmed milk. Add the crumbs and the yolks. Last of all, add the stiff beaten egg whites. Bake in a soufflé pan or a baking dish.

Shirred Crabs
½ lb crab
4 oz. butter
6 oz. bread crumbs
3 eggs
1 cup milk
onion, parsley, pepper and salt

Stir this mixture together and then add the crab, tasting as you go.

Grandmother's Boston Cookies

1 cup butter

1½ cup sugar

4 eggs

3¼ cups flour

1 cup sun-dried raisins

1 cup chopped nuts

1 teaspoon cinnamon

1 teaspoon cloves

1 teaspoon baking soda dissolved in hot water

Mix together: the mixture will be stiff. Drop by teaspoons on greased baking sheet. Bake in medium oven about fifteen minutes, or until the cookies are crisp and brown.

Charlie Johnson's Sponge Cake

4 eggs

1 cup sugar

1 cup flour

1 lemon

Beat yolks with sugar until very light; then beat whites stiff, and fold them into the yolk and sugar mixture. Add the flour. Cook immediately, about twenty minutes at medium temperature.

Sally Lunn Muffins

2 cups flour

1 cup milk

2 eggs

1 tablespoon of lard or butter

2 teaspoons baking powder

1 teaspoon full sugar

Mix lightly and bake in a medium to hot oven, about thirty minutes.

Grandmother would make a caramel cake (the icing sticky, the inside all dark yellow and comforting), or a Lane cake filled with raisins and nuts, drenched in bourbon. When the parts around the pecans in the filling started to go brown, you just had to wrap it in damp cheesecloth. It changed your mood entirely.

Actually, it was with Grandmother that I had my first and only mint julep: I think it was to celebrate my having done that first oil painting of a magnolia, sensual, and looking very much as if it wanted to be painted by Georgia O'Keeffe. Not that it had been, but you could tell it would have liked that. Grandmother didn't have a recipe, just a light hand with it, as with everything. Here is a recipe for mint julep from Walker Percy, who called it his favorite:

Cud'n Walker's Uncle Will's Favorite Mint Julep Receipt

You need excellent Bourbon whiskey; rye or Scotch will not do. Put half an inch of sugar in the bottom of the glass and merely dampen it with water. Next, very quickly—and here is the trick in the procedure— crush your ice, actually powder it, preferably in a towel with a wooden mallet, so quickly that it remains dry, and, slipping two sprigs of fresh mint against the inside of the glass, cram the ice in right to the brim, packing it in with your hand. Finally, fill the glass, which apparently has no room left for anything else, with Bourbon, the older the better, and grate a bit of nutmeg on the top. The glass will frost immediately. Then settle back in your chair for half an hour of cumulative bliss.

We did settle in for that bliss, Grandmother and I. I notice there is nutmeg here, as there was in many things growing up in the South. I still love shaking it over whatever seems to call for it.

Grandmother loved most to teach all of us and our friends how to do things properly. She would have ten of us over for dinner around a lace tablecloth with forks and knives of different lengths and different-shaped spoons. One would be used first for her own fiery black bean bisque with sherry and lemon, another later for her homemade peach ice cream so rich it would leave a coating against the metal ice tray, so fresh that the bits of freestone peach were all straggly in it.

She would show us about the finger bowl, how to dip our fingers just to the first knuckle in the water with the tiny orange nasturtium blossom floating on top. When a friend of mine took a swallow of the water, we all laughed except Grandmother, who never laughed at anyone, except sometimes herself.

Not that I was receptive to everything about Grandmother, especially her views on southern wisdom. She would invite me into her enormous too-soft bed where I would feel smothered. I'd sink to the middle and feel miserable. Here it was that she would talk to me about Life. One thing about it was you were never to let out anything once confided in you: gossip would run wild if you started it. This warning was accompanied with some German verse she would recite with convincing gestures about a bird escaping from a cage—apart from the Vogel whose feathers would fly away so that it would never come back, I cannot remember anything at all of the poem. I was cautious enough for a while though, except with Peg, of course.

Life for Grandmother was especially about how you were supposed always to flatter men young and old, always beginning with the topic of their ties. This was uncontroversial and did not show off your brains. Sugar catches more flies than vinegar, said Grandmother with a little laugh, amused by the cliché, yet believing it all the same. I resisted saying I didn't care too much for flies, or that I wasn't planning to catch anyone anyway, I wanted to live an artistic life. I'm sure she knew all that. But she somehow had managed to do that and the southern part too.

I have had to admit that Grandmother may have had a point about life. One of the boring girls who was a great social success was Lula. I thought of her as Lula-the-dumb. I never liked her, with her wavy hair and liquid brown eyes—quite like a cow, I thought. Anyway, Lula was proof positive that the tie conversation works, because she surely didn't have any other. Lula would bat her eyelashes, roll her immense eyes around, and men felt admired. I was amazed, and I disliked Lula. She earned an A in home economics for growing perfect fingernails after biting them for years. I earned a C minus by making, from some parachute silk sent to me by my uncle Devereux from China a pair of pajamas that kept falling to pieces, and I have never stopped biting my nails. Lula's mother would not let her get wet in the ocean above her knees, drink from a Coca-Cola bottle, eat ice cream after oysters or any other seafood, or ride in the front seat of a car. She was *very* careful. It all worked for Lula, a superbly detestable example of southern wisdom, who married young, and stayed that way—married and young. If she was perhaps smarter than she let on, that was part of her smartness. I just hadn't figured it out.

Grandmother's stories were the opposite of Mother's. You felt right there, part of them.

I am riding with her at top speed over the steppes in Russia in a troika, a fur stole flung over us as the driver holds us in; I am dining with her in France from a gold service, given by Napoleon to someone whose descendants she knows. I am strapping myself, like Turner, to the mast of a ship in a storm to observe it, and later to paint it just as she did. I am as energetic and resourceful as she is, while I listen to her. I am her kind of southern; I am strong as long as no one knows it, and I feel I can weather anything as long as I am with her.

Grandmother always knew what was more important and what was less so; she never confused them. Even when she would lose her keys, looking lost herself, her face would suddenly beam when she would look at you. She would ask you to sit down by her and tell her everything. Wasn't that what we all needed, someone to sit down by?

It was in what I thought of as my grandmother's mountains that I first climbed on a horse, slowly walking with the stirrup boy beside, or Ginny the teacher, with her firm thin face and blond hair gleaming. Later, on camp trips, a horse blind in one eye stumbled with me clinging on, along the mountain side of the trail while I held my breath. The burning coffee in the tin cups, searing our lips, and the hot biscuits over the fire made up for the fright.

One early Sunday morning, we had gone to pick some yellow flowers: we must have disturbed a nest because, apparently from nowhere, a dozen yellow jackets suddenly swarmed upon me, and I fainted. To this day, I take shots for the allergic reaction triggered by them, by wasps, or yellow-faced hornets. Like some plague visited on me by that same God that killed my puppy, gave me a father always in pain, a mother too beautiful.

I am at my grandmother's cottage in Linville, with its deep chestnut walls and its smell of wood smoke from her getting up early and lighting the fire before going to her easel. I have chosen mushroom instead of vegetable soup, and Nunny is pointing out to me how much more expensive it is. How can I always judge things so wrongly?

I remember our long walks past the sunstruck slopes hiding the tiny strawberries, making our way slowly toward the shade of the poisonous rhododendrons on the other side of the mountain. Peg and I would gather glossy clumps of galax leaves, stacking them in clumps to take home to the house wrapped in fog. Dew glistened in the early morning on the blue forget-me-nots in the ditch. Lizards sunned themselves on the wall by the studio. Salamanders appeared orange in the sunlight and then changed color on the rough stones. Grandmother's paintings with their rich still lifes of copper gleaming and ginger pots, statues, and strewn flowers, hung familiarly on the walls.

FAMILY LIFE

It was in the Linville mountains in Little Switzerland that I was sent to camp As You Like It. I didn't much. We all wore white shorts on Sundays, blue shorts the rest of the time, and devoured molasses and biscuits, corn bread, honey, and hot chocolate.

How fat you are!

exclaimed Father after one summer, when we were at the beach again.

Oh dear, am I? I'm sorry,

I said.

Father is rocking on the porch of our beach cottage, with a rhythm that the boards magnify—crk-Crk, crk-Crk—and looking out over the water. I wish I knew just something about him, but don't know how to ask. What was it like growing up here; what were his parents like; what does he wish he could be doing; will he ever be able to do it? I wonder if Mother knows any of this. I never see them talking together, have never seen them touch.

When he comes home, I am supposed to go out to kiss him welcome. I'd rather not, so I pretend I'm thoroughly involved in practicing the piano.

Most of all, I liked being sick. I would get cambric tea, very weak with lots of milk, and lie in bed and read. Mother would give up her appointments:

I have canceled *everything* for you, dear.

Then she would sit down by me and tell me stories about Europe and being a little girl there. Peg preferred to get sick at Christmas so she wouldn't have to go and stand in the circle of radiant faces around the tree at the parish house and sing.

> *All four of us are playing quadruple solitaire at home. These are the best times. Mother concentrates hard and always slaps her cards down first when there is a chance; she loves playing anything. Father is humming something under his breath. I think he looks very dapper. Peg is in her fuzzy sweater, tapping her foot in excitement. No one could resist Peg when she is in a good mood. I burst out: "What a great family!" and then feel embarrassed.*

After Grandmother's plantation house by the water had been sold and the Linville cottage given away, it was the turn of our beach cottage at Wrightsville. I went back to look at that porch and the sound below, where the pale-colored sandfiddlers had scuttled about with their big claw menacing until they got to their hole in the sand. It was on the porch of that house that Father had looked for so long at so many sunsets. He used to look down for a long time at his boat, moored to the pier. I wondered if he had ever loved anything so much as that boat. He would look at it more than at us. He seemed less bored at the beach. That flat expanse of water must have given some mirror to his thoughts. I don't think any of us, even Mother, ever knew what they were.

I was never much of a hit in Wilmington, at dates or at dances, and found the country club where the dances were held a torment. We went sometimes on Sunday after church and had to sit with people we were supposed to know, because we always had. I always forgot everyone's names, especially the ladies who wore too much lipstick so it left traces on my cheek or chin. Mother, whose lipstick you would scarcely notice, would wipe the red off my cheek with her handkerchief, moistening it on her tongue.

Inside the large dining room there stood in the place of honor a mountainous slab of roast beef, which no one liked rare but me. The jellied salads quivered on either side of it, waiting for us, with some dreary cold shrimp in aspic. To get the right dessert, you had to be rapid while you looked nonchalant. The lemon tart was tangy; the coconut cake was fragrant; the chocolate mousse had no taste. There was never any pecan pie.

I liked it best when Mother would go to the country club dances like the L'Ariosa, because she would always bring home little cakes for Peg and me, wrapped up in silver paper or tiny gold boxes. But eventually, I had to go to such dances myself. I was right to dread it. One dance, for the "spinsters," took place annually while I was growing up. You went until you were a spinster no more. I think I would have gotten married just to avoid it. Perhaps I did.

I see myself, in the picture kept on my mother's kidney-shaped desk, on the right of the embossed leather part. Later, looking at the desk, I think of how Thomas Aquinas had such a semicircle carved out of his too, to accommodate his largish tummy: I always liked him for that. In the picture, I am standing, awkward and plump in a strapless green dress, a green carnation taped to my bare skin above it. Your escort would call the day before, inquire about the tint of your dress, and place his flower order. If this strapless green costume didn't look like me, nothing else really seemed to either. Dances I loathed. I had to go with the boy next door who felt himself assigned to me by his parents and mine. He was going on to another party afterward, and I wasn't. Mother had laid out fruitcake on the good plates for us, as she always did, and he wouldn't be stopping to have any.

There never was a dance floor I didn't feel absurd on. If Mother and Father were there, moving effortlessly about chatting with everyone and keeping an eye on me, I would feel more and more awkward. I would dance with Bishop Wright, my family's close friend. His face was sweet, and he had endless patience, but I just knew he was as bored as I was ungainly. I was never going to get gainly. The pink and green camellia-shaped ice cream, always too hard, skidded across the plate onto my dress of awful and shiny green satin.

I'm sorry,

I said to my date, who had been sent to relieve the bishop so he could dance with his other parishioners. I knew I was messing up the dance steps on the glossy floor.

Don't come to me with your troubles,

he said. This was thought of in those days as a very funny rejoinder. Spencer was very funny. I was relieved when it was the finale and everyone danced slowly and sort of nestled into each other's cheeks and chests. Not me.

My date was supposed to take me home; you could only get in or out one side of his car. He had you trapped if he wanted to make a move at you. He wouldn't be planning to move over at me anyway, I knew that. In any case, he was positively delighted to take me home, so he could go off on his own. Of course, I knew he would never have been coming in, but I couldn't have told Mother that. I took the fruitcake off the silver plate, wrapped it up in foil to keep it fresh, had a glass of milk, went upstairs, and pulled the tape off the carnation, which I threw away. Then I climbed into bed between my piled-up books, pushing them aside to make room.

If I had been with someone more companionable, we would probably have preferred to raid the icebox than have fruitcake off our best plates. As it was, I usually came in alone and had to put away the little snack so carefully prepared. It was all fraught with concern. The few times I did go out with someone I might have liked, Father would wait at the door in case he might have wanted to kiss me. If we were late, Mother would be pacing up and down, sometimes Nunny pacing with her. I'd not have minded having the cake with them but that never happened. Things for guests were for guests.

SAVANNAH

When the war broke out, Father turned his white hair yellowish with Grecian Formula, lied about his age, and went off to drive an ambulance with the Eighth Army in Italy. He was legally too old, but that was not lying, it was showing guts.

One day I took my ten-cent allowance and bought a candy bar. This was frivolous and shocked Mother. "During the war, darling?" I didn't try to explain how I felt. I don't know exactly why. Father sent us some V-letters, with so many things crossed out by the censors that I could barely read what was left.

I was a misfit in Savannah, Georgia, where I was sent to be with the

Lippitt family, my mother's elder brother, Max, and his wife, Mary. I had to be away from home, for Mother was being unwell. I stayed with my debutante-age cousin Ashby in Savannah for what seemed a very long time indeed. She was supposed to get me dates; I reacted badly, disliking things to be planned for me. In their enormous house on Drayton Street, with its marble hall and stately staircase, the rooms all seemed very large. Nothing was ever out of place but me. I never felt at home, no matter how hard everyone tried. They were social beings, kind and immensely distinguished, never arguing, never losing their tempers.

My aunt Mary was short and stately. Regal in posture, with her head thrown back and to the side, moving in a stately fashion about the marble halls in a muted tweed suit and low-heeled leather pumps, perfectly shined. She was gracious and I was petrified; we stayed that way. Once when my cousin Maxie shot me with a BB gun (for fun, as he later said) I screamed in panic, and my aunt was displeased. Mother said that when Aunt Mary had fallen off a horse, which then rolled on her, she never even cried. She got right up and walked home. Of course.

> Darling, said Aunt Mary to me one gray day, darling, have you noticed the difference in the blue of your blouse and your skirt? It doesn't matter in the slightest, of course. But I know your dear mother would want me to ask.

I thought a minute to see if I had noticed, decided I had not, and looked down at my blouse. It was a dusty blue because my cousin had said it went with my eyes. Did my skirt go with it? Well, probably not. My dear mother would certainly have thought not.

> No, ma'am, I guess it doesn't, does it?

But in fact what was I expected to do, go up and change? Be polite, Mary Ann, you are here on sufferance, I said to myself.

> Not at all, my dear. Why don't you just go do whatever you were about to do? I certainly wouldn't want to interrupt you. It was really just for my information. A matter of no importance whatsoever.

I put on my long trench coat to cover the offending colors and dashed out to the garden to sulk and to play with the Pekinese, Ling, who wouldn't notice. Pekinese are always well dressed. The August heat was smudgy. Steam was rising from the rose beds, and my trench coat was stifling me. A smell of cooking rutabagas made the air pungent. I knew there was rhubarb and green apple pie for dessert, because I had gone behind the swinging door to chat with Mattie the cook about this and that, and she showed me.

My uncle Max was tall and intellectual looking, with piercing brown eyes and a smallish nose, the nostrils flaring out like those of a horse. A good horseman himself, he liked mostly to give me books on every imaginable subject, earnestly inquiring later what I had thought of them. I was amazed he wanted to know. No one in my family would have asked me.

As for the relationship of my aunt and uncle, I hadn't any clear idea, although I studied them hard when they were at the opposite ends of the very long table. They didn't argue, they conversed, as we were supposed to. Aunt Mary would always sit near the kitchen, with a little bell under the blue and red Persian carpet she would press to summon the maid. Uncle Max, at the other end where he could carve and serve the wine, always dressed for dinner, with a tie and a clean white shirt.

I was often cramped for fear in that house. Mrs. Cowan, my great-aunt and the grande dame of the family, would be sitting straight upright upstairs, near the little elevator they had put in for her. She could look out on the courtyard with its roses. I would be summoned in periodically for her to see what progress I might be making in the life of the mind. One day I had to report on Nevil Shute's *On the Beach* and its political stance. Alas, what did I know, after all?

> *I remember little squares of hominy grits fried and crunchy, cold melon slices served with little spoons. Orange juice and peanuts before my cousin's piano lessons, to which she has to take me. We walk through the quiet squares of Old Savannah, past the houses where she knows everyone, past the gardens and the shade trees.*

Ashby's piano teacher seemed to listen to what she was playing, which I found impressive. At home, as I would be laboring through Debussy and Bach, Scottie, my portly teacher and the organist in church, would always be listening to something through his headphones as I played. A ball game, a concert, so it didn't matter how many mistakes I made.

With Ashby, I attended the Pape School, where everyone seemed to write that cursive script with elegant letters swooping into each other, as if they were printed. I never managed this, but people were very kind.

After my adenoids were taken out, I had plate after plate of smooth ice cream, all the books I could read, brought into my room by Uncle Max, mostly Albert Payson Terhune's books about horses and dogs, and on the small gramophone there, I could listen to Rachmaninoff and Bartok, in recordings of Arthur Rubenstein, a friend of the family who used to play the grand piano in the marble hall. That was the nicest part of the visit.

There are endless debutante parties, under the tall oaks and moss, with champagne of different colors: pink, green, and ordinary yellowish. Camellias on the lawns in white and pink, azaleas in bursting blooms of loud magenta. At someone's plantation, spun sugar baskets for dessert at every place, place cards hand colored, a tiny marigold glued to each. The profusion everywhere gives me a lonely feeling.

COMING HOME

When you get home after a while away, things look odd. Funny what you hadn't seen before. The old houses in town with their paint peeling off were like our sunburns when we were little. We would use tea compresses to make them better. Something was always going wrong you couldn't make any better. Nunny would always understand, even if she couldn't help.

Father came home too, from the war. He brought me a Scottish cap, navy blue with a fold in it so you could turn it around, to wear it either way. It had a little insignia on it to remind me of our background. I couldn't have forgotten anyway. Donald MacDonald came every year to the Blue Ridge Mountains around Linville for the Highland Games, and our friends the Mortons and the MacRaes had built little Scottish houses called Dunvegan and the like. At the games, Peg took a picture of me in that cap, and a plaid skirt in our tartan, MacDonald of the Isle of Skye. I am looking away.

The war hero who Father had been was hard to reach. He was as difficult and silent as he was upstanding and scrupulous. When he was little, he had walked five miles to pay back a coin he had borrowed. When he had been "naughty," he would write a letter of self-blame to his aunt, whom he called

"Darling" all his life. He had never been known to swear or to lie. Mother told us several times about all this. He was both admirable and far away.

About personal beliefs he would not answer if I asked, as I made the mistake of doing once, only once. Surely, I thought, I could one day find a topic sufficiently impersonal for him to discuss it with me. When he got back home from the war, he felt very different. He took me to see Anna Magnani in *Open City*. In the torture scene, I gagged my mouth so I couldn't scream. He said he wanted us to know about things, exactly all those things he couldn't talk about. In our bookcases and lying on his table, there were books with pictures of war casualties and torture methods left around. I think he might have been tortured, but I try not to think about it. I believe he was in the OSS and carried poison under his fingernails so he wouldn't give information away if he was caught and questioned.

At the words "starving" or "suffering," or at the sight of a child crying, he would weep openly. If any of us ever said we were hungry, his anger would explode. We could not possibly know about hunger, about pain. Once when his plane had been shot down and he parachuted into a marshy spot of quicksand, a fable of a little frog beating the cream he was drowning in to butter was what he clung to. He kicked so hard he stayed afloat until he was saved by a French peasant woman.

Always he was in pain from three broken ribs and a pin in the hip of his right leg, the shorter one. And from a later accident long after both wars he served in, when he was traveling between towns; he was found lying under a truck where he must have been for hours. He was brought back with what he called a cauliflower ear and the broken hip: I can hear the ambulance siren right now. . . . He preferred continuous discomfort to having a stiffened leg.

But he never told us war stories as I supposed other fathers did, even when we got up the courage to ask. Mother said he could make you think he was a native of any country, could use his knife and fork the right way for wherever he was, that he spoke several languages, Polish, French, and some others. It seemed as if all this brought him nothing but memories of pain. He spoke mostly about others, like his buddy Merion Cooper, who made *King Kong* long after.

Father would go out to the sunporch and listen to records of Marlene Dietrich singing "Lili Marlene." If you went out to listen with him, he would turn it off. We supposed he just had to be alone. Here was a picture of him in the hall, his chest sticking out and his chin high, being decorated by a man in a top hat with a great white moustache. This was Jan Paderewski in Poland, Mother said, because he had volunteered for the Kosciusko squadron before being shot down. I played some of Paderewski's music in tribute, but softly, because Mother said Father didn't like to hear the piano much these days. I guess he would always have preferred to hear Marlene Dietrich singing "Lili Marlene."

Once, I figured if I asked him, he would tell me if there was something he might have wanted to talk about. This was the only time I dared to ask. You can't just plunge into something nobody gives you an opening for. One day he was sitting there in the pantry at the little table all by himself with his thermos of coffee Mother had fixed him. She must have tried many times to talk with him, but maybe the phone would have rung in the middle of it, or she would have had something she had to do for someone. You could tell her mind wasn't with you a lot of the time, even when she would ask you to tell her something, because she knew you wanted to talk about it. It's not like Grandmother who had time to hear. I thought if Father had anything he could or would tell, he would have wanted whoever was listening to be there, right there. Anything he would have had to tell would have had complications to it.

I see us sitting for what seems like hours, in our small pantry, on two little white wooden benches across from each other with the table between. Father's hip is hurting; he follows every bit of the news, fascinated:

Oh,

he is saying to Mother,

Mrs. Cardwell served those funny things in tomato aspic to her ladies for bridge. Did you know her brother? He used to come to the club.

It's pretty wonderful, now that I think back over it, that he should have wanted to keep up even with that.

I wanted to try to reach him one day, so I went to sit across from him and just looked at him and the jug of coffee until he looked up.

How come you're not in school? he asked.
Saturday. No school on Saturday.
What can I do for you? he asked, sort of flat.

How in the world was I going to do this?

> Well, I said, you know I haven't any notion of what it's like to do all sorts of things you've done, and I wondered . . .

I paused and didn't know how to go on. I'd forgotten to put the "sir" in so he would know I wasn't being uppity or anything. He didn't look angry exactly, not friendly either. I guess he was just not used to anyone asking. Getting this far, I had to go on.

> Like in the first war you were in, when you went up to drop bombs and you got shot at through the helmet, but they missed because you were short, and when you had to parachute into the quicksand and saved yourself by some story or other.
> I guess your mother told you about some of those things, did she?
> Yes sir, but I'd love to hear the details.

It was probably the best thing I had ever done up to that point. Father told me about what it was like to look down at the enemy lines when you had to destroy something. What it was like to be in danger of drowning, and how he had remembered the tale of the little frog, and how the French woman had found him. How he hoped if I ever went over there, I would try to find her, in L'Hay-les-Roses, where she lived, to thank her for him.

I never felt so close to him as that morning. At one point, he pushed the bench back from the table and asked if I would like to go up to the attic with him to see some things.

> Of course, I said, when?
> Now, unless there's something else you'd rather be doing?
> No sir, I'd really like that.

So up we went, from the pantry to the next floor, and then up the steep stairs to the attic where all his war things were gathered, from wherever he'd been, like a museum. When I'd been up there alone before, it had always felt vacant, like a memory that might not want to be remembered.

This time was different. His face took on another sort of look there. Not sad, just thoughtful. I studied all those posters in red and black from the First World War, with pictures of him in his fighter planes, with helmet and goggles, sitting upright. He looked different from the way he did now, prouder, straighter.

I'd heard from Mother how he'd been decorated many times in many countries, just the kind of thing he wouldn't talk about. He would change the subject about those years and those memories so quickly you wouldn't know you had asked, unless you felt your face flushing, the way mine did. This time again in the attic, like the times I had gone up alone before, I saw the little tin container that I remembered, with his medals all jumbled up with different coins. As if he had put it all away together, period.

But this morning felt unusual: all the time, he was looking at me and then the pictures. Like he hadn't seen me before, like I didn't have to worry about not being the son he'd always hoped for. What I really wanted to see were things from his time as a spy in the OSS—Mother said he had carried strange items here and there, found out various secrets, been on perilous expeditions, spoken many languages. I'd have liked to hear it from him.

That wasn't to be.

Suddenly, when he was bending over something I think he was about to show me, Mother called from downstairs about making plans. They both liked making plans, I suppose. Father's face closed back to the way I was used to it, that light went out in his eyes, and he headed back down the steps.

Those steps were high and hard for him because of his bad hip, although he never complained. As for what he might have gone on to say, it's not as important as our having been together up there alone.

Sometimes I would be sent upstairs in a hurry, and the voices below would sound louder than usual, echoing strangely in the halls with the high ceilings. Sometimes Father would leave the house in a huff, over something I would never know. Once I was sent to bring him back; I didn't manage to.

Father disapproved of pets after the war: they must have seemed frivolous to him. He probably disapproved of a great deal but didn't talk about it. Apart from taking trips together, the best thing was quadruple solitaire or gin rummy we could all play, or our late-night ritual of hot toddies for all of us, with just a little bourbon, lots of milk and sugar, and nutmeg over the top, I was the one who shook the nutmeg out of the container, and I would give everyone a lot. When Father drank with all of us, it was as if we could join with him in something.

Maybe you just never grow up at home. Too much past. I could never use the telephone without Mother reminding me in a whisper to thank somebody for something or asking me afterward if I did.

Why don't you phone . . . ?

I froze always, hating the sound of my voice on the telephone or anyone else's.

> *I am about ten. I am supposed to be selling subscriptions to the school magazine, asking our family friends. So I phone Miss Jocelyn, whose number Mother gives me, and explain it all to her. Well, our school is putting out a magazine and we are supposed to get subscriptions from our family's friends, and I thought of you right away. It's ten dollars for the whole year and you get nine issues, I think. The money goes to the orphanage downtown, isn't that nice?*
> *You will? That's super. Thanks so much, Miss Jocelyn.*
> *I am pleased with myself and my mother's friends, and treat myself to a little hum. Mother is not pleased: I seem to have been speaking too rapidly and was "unnecessarily quick" to get off the phone. It wouldn't surprise me if she phoned Miss Jocelyn afterward to apologize for me. I am trying to learn to speak for myself, and Miss Jocelyn and I have always gotten along just fine.*

Letters were worse than the telephone even; how could I be trusted to say the right thing? Especially to a young man. Even when I was relatively grown up, in high school, I didn't seem to do things right.

> *I am writing to Leslie in my class about a presentation we have to do.*

What are you going to say to him, dear?
I don't have any notion until I write it, Mother.

Not polite, Mary Ann. But I am annoyed. It's not over:

Oh, do take your time, dear. When you are done, perhaps you'd like me to take a look just to see . . .
To see what?
Well, you know, if the tone is right. You know.

Well, I don't know, don't want to know. I go in my room with my letter and finish it.

Then I feel dreadful. My mother and all. I come out to say I am sorry, which I'm not.

Mother, I was rude. I'm sorry.
That's all right, dear. I didn't mean to be intrusive. I just thought perhaps I could be of some use. I only wanted to give you some pointers. But don't worry about it. I was wrong to try to help. Mothers get it all upside down so often, don't they, dear?

Wow. Give me a break. What can I say? I give her the letter.

Darling, is that really what you want to say?

What had I said? What had I said? I mail the letter without reading it over. Would she have tried to help Peg with a letter or is it just me?

When Peg came home for vacation from Hollins College, where she went after National Cathedral, we would go every morning down to the beach, to walk out on the pier over the ocean before anyone else was up. Holding our flimsy cups of hot coffee gingerly, we would walk out on the wooden slats just warming up. One of them halfway out had been loose as long as I could remember, sticking up sideways, with its rusty nails showing. Once, Peg tried to hammer it down with her left shoe while I watched the slight waves moving under it noiselessly. Then she smiled at me and left it as it was. That seemed right.

We would always say hi to the fishermen and they would grin back. Often, several large mackerel would be already flopping back and forth on the pier, their scales shiny in the rising light. We liked to perch on one of the high benches to chat, putting our paper cups on the weathered slab of the baiting table in front of us. With the fall coming on, it might be a bit crisp, even on one of those days when the afternoon would quiver bright in the sun, as if it would last forever. You could smell the sea and the fish at once.

Little by little, the sky would go from pink to blue white, and the water would get that green we loved on it. No noise but the small whirr of the fishermen's rods casting out and an occasional exclamation. Sometimes we would talk, and sometimes just look at the ocean and think our own thoughts or remember.

We could talk about anything, Peg and I. Why Father drank so much— because he was in pain, we decided—and why Mother often seemed so sad. What we'd do later. Why the air at home hung so heavy, especially at supper, with Father eating his soup so slowly and Mother looking like she wished he'd finish so she could clear things up. I used to wonder if other families had conversation at mealtimes, the way we didn't.

Sometimes we'd remember about that terrible time we'd almost drowned, just the two of us, swimming alone. We'd heard all our lives about not going out over your head in the ocean, but it hadn't sunk in until then. We had been taking an ordinary swim. It was getting late, but the water wasn't cold yet. We weren't thinking about being out too far; we were just where we usually were. The sun was setting on the water, pink on green with a gold tinge. It was September, and you could see some little jellyfish washed up.

There was a strong undertow. I noticed it around my ankles. Just when I was about to yell at Peg to watch out, I was suddenly pulled in over my head, like something grabbing me and tugging harder than I could resist. When I finally caught sight of Peg, I could tell right away from her face that she couldn't touch bottom either. Her face had gone whitish green, and she was making that sound she makes when she's scared, just repeating the same syllable over and over, loud and then soft, soft and then loud. Now she was sort of waving her arms at me and shouting something I couldn't hear. We were both out where we couldn't touch, just the way you dread being in your dreams. When we finally managed to drag ourselves in, I was still so terrified I could feel my teeth chattering. I guess we liked remembering this because it made us feel rescued from something, and by ourselves.

When one day out on the pier I told Peg about Mother and my letter, she just kept looking at the water. I couldn't tell what she was thinking. She has always been so loyal that I knew she wasn't going to want to say anything bad about Mother, no matter what.

Do you feel terrible about it?

she asked me, looking at the water so I wouldn't feel funny. Peg sometimes used to talk to me about forgiving people, nothing gooey, just straightforward. I guess she's had to forgive a lot in her time, about others and also me.

Later it was getting hotter, and we hadn't said anything else. Then Peg told me something awful she had to do once. I knew it felt joined for her to my letter episode. When she was little, Peg believed in the Easter Bunny and Santa Claus. Me, I don't know when I stopped believing, but Peg was the one who kept her eyes closed in that picture. And Mother wanted Peg to stop believing, who knows why?

So she had it set up that Peg would have to catch Father in his Santa outfit, and that would take care of it all. Peg would see it was about parental love and not some mysterious thing or other. Peg was supposed to sit up late and then surprise Santa behind the sofa. Terrified, she did it, hating it as much as Father did. They did what you did in our family about awkward things. Maybe all families, I don't know. You just never said anything about it again, as if it had never been there.

How could Mother ever have dreamed that up? Peg had nightmares for a long time about it. Maybe Father did too: we didn't know him well enough to ask.

I tried to get near people, but it seldom felt right. When I was in New Hanover High, someone in my class was called C.R.: who knows what it stood for. It didn't matter to me at all, because nothing about him aroused my curiosity. He seemed more polite than smart, but I was missing Peg and our chats. He came from the right sort of parents for mine to approve of him. Mother was delighted to see me with someone so proper.

It couldn't have worked, though. C.R. was always dressed the right way for whatever occasion it happened to be: golf shoes for golf, Top Siders for sailing, tux for formal things, and understated dull jackets for quiet evenings. He didn't have to think about it, he just did it. An admirable trait, surely. But something about his utter predictability left me chilly. When Mother persuaded me to give a "pirate party," C.R. came home with me, having cut off a new pair of khakis with just the right jagged edges. Actually, the people I might have preferred always looked dressed for a pirate party without cutting off their new pants.

You couldn't get more opposite to me as I really was or thought I was than C.R. With it all, he was incredibly polite. When he went to church in his good jacket, he sat with his family on the second row to the left of the central aisle, visibly paid attention to the minister giving the sermon, didn't wince at grammatical mistakes, and was very serious about church as about every-thing else. He never turned around to look at anything or anyone. C.R. was destined to be a lawyer, and at one point I asked what sort of law he liked.

Corporation law,

he said to me. It sounded very solemn. He repeated it in case I hadn't gotten it. I got it, but wasn't sure what it was and didn't care enough to ask. When C.R. went away to law school, I was still in Wilmington at New Hanover High. He worked very hard, as he always had. I didn't, but I hoped he hadn't noticed. We would set out on dates, him with his torts case book in a large green folder in case there was time to spare. He would take out a thick yellow marker and highlight at least one-third of every page. Maybe it was that habit that signaled the death of us even as a potential couple. I would make a thin pencil line down the margin of the parts of whatever book I was reading that I wanted to remember. As I reasoned, if you can call it that, our marking differently meant we were bound to be thinking differently; indeed we were.

Years later, when I had gone away to college, after prep school, I continued to see C.R. when I came home. He was a friend, stiff, not very smart, but a friend. Until, one day C.R. cleared his throat and proposed to me:

C.R.: What about getting married?
Me: Do what?
C.R.: I said I think we might perhaps get married.
Me: Mmm . . .
C.R.: Lots of us are getting hitched these days, you know, all my fra-ternity brothers. We are all going to stay real close. You aren't going to mind that, are you?
Me: Oh. sure. Fine. Of course not.

If our own relationship went nowhere after that, he at least had his mates.

Over those high school years before I went away, there was also the rather prim and angular Tommy. He was intensely British, had a strong sense of hierarchy, a talent for writing, and a mysterious family life. That was four marks in his favor, as far as I was concerned. He would read to me from large volumes, verses from Robert Louis Stevenson or somebody about the crescent moon and someone's slipping a bridle from his hand, because he was bound by his heart and that hand, and what had to rhyme with it, what else but: "the queen of fairyland."

That's you,

he said.

Oh,

I said. I didn't feel like that. But Tommy would sit on my front doorstep much of the night to prove he was fond of me. That was after Father had closed the door on him, because we might have kissed. We wouldn't have, because Tommy parted his hair in the middle. It was never going to work between us, which I might have known from that detail—but it took me a while to figure this out. Not paying a lot of attention to anything, I was lost in my own past or in whatever book I was living in. Tommy would ask me questions like

What do you want to do tonight?

And I would answer, dumb but determined, that I wanted to do everything. Tommy would stay serious:

We can't do everything, you know, Mary Ann. We can do only one or two things. I am saying you can choose those.

Now I knew you couldn't do everything, but I certainly wanted to. One of the best things we did was to go out, a few of us, to the Maco Light, a railroad track about an hour away. You waited and sang and hoped you might see the figure of a rail man who had lost his head coming back to look for it, swinging his lantern. After a while, we'd drive home.

Collective things were easier than anything one-to-one. Bobby (Blaine Browne, or Blaine Butler as he was later to call himself), my only artistic boyfriend, who would come visiting often from his home in Pennsylvania, was used to seating himself at my piano, his voluminous black cape swirling about him, and thunder on the keys. Then he broke the sounding board, left in confusion, and did not return for a long while.

Atop that piano I kept the picture of my photogenic youngest uncle from Savannah, in a naval uniform. I would tell anyone who inquired that he was my boyfriend, away somewhere. Nearby, an ivory bridge arched over a black lacquer table, with seven elephants marching over it. They never seemed to stumble, the way I stumbled over the ivory keys and much else.

HOLDING HOME TOGETHER

Two things held us symbolically as a family. First, the hot toddies we would all four stand in a circle to drink; Father would always ask me to shake the nutmeg on the sugary mixture of milk and bourbon. I'd do it with a heavy hand and a light heart. And the second was Nunny's custard. She would prepare it whenever something was wrong somewhere. Either she sensed it or she knew it would happen. You couldn't forget its taste ever, sweet and comforting, with the nutmeg I would shake on the top, sprinkling those uneven brown dots here and there. It smelled warm, like the kitchen.

Nunny must have talked to us at those times, Peg and me, when Mother and Father had gone upstairs. She would guess whatever was wrong, with her large smile we loved so much, her teeth sparkling in her dark face under a brown paper bag or a white kerchief over her sister's "transformation" she wore always. I believe her own hair had turned red. But that's not what I remember exactly, just the nutmeg smell and the feeling it would be all right, whatever we lost or missed. Whatever happened.

One thing I never managed to talk about, but it sticks in my mind. It happened at our beach cottage at Wrightsville, where so much had always taken place.

> *Mother and I are chatting on the porch, about supper and what we'll have. A car pulls up and a so-called friend of the family steps out. My mother's face goes bright red; this friend is the one she thinks Father is involved*

with. Still, you have to be hospitable in the South. My mother invites her in for a drink, and I go get out our best glasses, the green ones with crackles going up and down. I didn't have to ask, I knew we'd use them, although we didn't very often.

Miss Susan asks for soda water, and we have none. I feel inadequate again. I have not been able to protect my mother, and we have fallen short in hospitality.

How could we have no soda water?

asks Mother afterward.

We should have.

I have been reflecting on this. To fall short is inexcusable, of one thing as another. We felt defenseless and inadequate: we had not had the presence of mind to have the soda water my father's friend desired. And we were at fault.

Many evenings, even after we had sold our cottage, I would go back to look at its porch and the sound below, where sandfiddlers scuttled about at low tide. Father had looked for so long at so many sunsets there, when he wasn't any longer so angry. We kept returning to Wrightsville Beach, our beach after all and in spite of everything.

Years after the soda water incident, on a summer day when we were in a tiny beach cottage we had rented in nostalgia for our lost one, Father fell from his bed onto the floor. I was there alone with him. He lay with his twisted neck on the floor, silent.

Don't let me take your time,

was all he said. Helpless, waiting for the ambulance, I still believed it was a question of interesting him, of calling him back from somewhere. What could I talk to him about?

No, I am not up to things.

He languished for three years with cancer in a nursing home. The only time he had to beg for morphine, the head nurse was having her Sunday lunch, and so he had to wait. I remember no grief at his death, glad he had to suffer no longer. Yet I see even now the way his chin juts out in front; mine does the same. I am my father's daughter.

Father had his habits. "You could make a meal out of soup," he would say every evening at suppertime, and so we began every evening meal with soup.

I still do: maybe I could have understood him now.

Two

Other Places

FOR PREP SCHOOL IN WASHINGTON, you had to have name tags on your clothes, red stitching on white. Mine said Mary Ann Rorison, and generally they were sewn right over the ones that said Margaret Lippitt Rorison, on the clothes Peg had outgrown. A little group of Mother's friends sat about, stitching and counseling me. There were a few bits of advice I might have done well to heed:

> Do please try not to grin, Mary Ann. It makes your cheeks so fat.
> Dear, couldn't you look less bored? Men will really hate your looking like that.
> You know, Mary Ann dear, you really shouldn't talk so fast; it makes people nervous.

It was Saturday, and the Metropolitan Opera was sounding from the radio: it was *Aida,* and I already felt strangled before the tomb scene. And by the name tags.

NATIONAL CATHEDRAL SCHOOL

At National Cathedral, you had to take a chaperone everywhere. I don't remember Mother and Peg mentioning this, but it surely stuck in my mind for years. Chaperoning even included visits to the dentist, after which you had to buy your escort whatever she wanted. Miss Pitchen, chosen to accompany me with her vacant smile, would sip her Broadway soda (chocolate ice cream, vanilla syrup) through a straw to make it last longer: *srr-srr-srr* it would go. I grew particularly to dislike ice cream sodas. When she ate the last remnants with the long spoon, there would be a little dab of the chocolate on the side of her mouth, right above her lipstick line—she wore "glorious rose," a color especially unsuited to her palish face.

Miss Pitchen had had a great disappointment in her life, I was told, and it had left her bitter and extremely fat. She loved to say her favorite phrase, which depressed me unutterably: "The only exercise that helps you lose weight is pushing away from the table." She would say this loudly and often, and since I was assigned to her table, I heard it a great deal. She could, with unerring aim, choose the exact moment when the justly celebrated dessert of the school, Cathedral Pudding, was brought to the table, its sauce all foamy and hot. I had absolutely no intention of pushing away from that table but did wish I had to go less often to the dentist.

Chef's Cathedral Pudding
An NCS tradition for many, many years!
Only served on special occasions.
1 pound shortening
2 pounds sugar
8 eggs
4 pounds bread flour
2½ pints milk
1 cup baking powder
¾ pound bitter chocolate
1½ teaspoons salt
¼ cup vanilla

Foamy Sauce:
½ pound butter
2 pounds confectioners' sugar
12 eggs, separated
½ pound granulated sugar
¼ cup vanilla
¾ cup hot water
Yellow coloring

Sift flour, baking powder, and salt. Cream shortening and sugar. Add eggs, one at a time while mixing. Add flour and milk alternately. Add melted chocolate and vanilla.

Fill 5 well-greased molds three-fourths full. Cover and steam 3 hours. Serve with foamy sauce.

Foamy Sauce:

Cream butter and confectioners' sugar. Add egg yolks, one at a time. Beat well. Place mixture in top of double boiler; add hot water. Stir over hot water until mixture is thick.

Beat egg whites until stiff and dry. Add granulated sugar a little at a time. Mix egg whites with first mixture while on heat. Add vanilla and a bit of yellow vegetable coloring. Beat well and remove from heat immediately.

Serves 50 generously.

National Cathedral School for Girls

Studies were important at this school, but so was one's religious upbringing. Math was taught by an elongated person called Miss Covey, with crinkly red hair standing up at odd angles all over, eyes that darted about, and hands that twitched nervously. She had, I suspect, a rather good mathematical brain, but seemed to keep it for herself. Neither I nor any of my classmates understood anything at all she put on the board, much of which she in any case erased with the back of her white button-up-to-the-neck blouse when she turned to face us. Our Bible teacher, whose name I have thank goodness forgotten, seemed peculiarly devoid of a sense of humor, and we teased her unmercifully. I loved the Latin teacher, who had braids on either side of her head, wound tightly in circles, and both English teachers: Miss Roberts, who read *The Bridge of San Luis Rey* with us and often to us, and Miss Hicks, who was in charge of the Drama Club and urged me to speak more slowly. I remember performing roles like the Old Man, in some play by Arthur Wing Pinero. It was certainly more fun than trying to declaim Juliet's monologue, coached by my mother, which I had had to do at New Hanover. Of that, I remember mostly "dashing out my desperate brains," raising my right arm about to do so: I found making any gesture awkward, and this was right up there with the worst. At Cathedral, I was fondest of practicing piano in the small studios downstairs right by the table where the milk and Uneeda biscuits were served in midmorning. And of singing hymns lustily in the Great Choir, looking at the Rose Window whenever I could. It appealed to me, as did singing. They were about the realest things of those years. Except for rolling down the grassy slope outside the cathedral: I did that often.

BRYN MAWR COLLEGE

From Cathedral, I went on to Bryn Mawr College, where Sarah Bird would be joining me the next year. In a women's college, it was said, you didn't have to compete with a masculine intelligence and a masculine speech. To me, it seemed to make absolutely no difference: my untimid classmates, no matter what gender, would have dominated anyway. Sydney de Shazo spoke long and well in our philosophy classes. I envied her that.

I never spoke at all in class, in any class. I was given voice lessons, so that my southern accent wouldn't stand in my way. But many other things seemed to. I didn't think myself much of a credit to Bryn Mawr when I was there: I couldn't imitate Rabelais or Montaigne, as Isabel, Ogden Nash's daughter could. I was a perpetual intermediate on the tennis court—all the Pem East students, Isabel and Anne and Caroline, were all advanced, and rightly so. Worst of all, I lacked the courage to even ask to study with Marianne Moore, whose poetry I adored and with whom I thought I had come to work.

Because I was determined to take philosophy, I was urged to take geology, as easier than physics, which seemed to me more naturally allied to philosophy and to me. I positively hated geology, the fossils, the whole thing, including the field trips when, since we were "roughing it," silt would dribble out of the taps with the water. My professor, Edward Watson I think his name was, was said to have married a bubble dancer; that seemed original to me. He had a wonderful smile, even if it happened to be directed more frequently at the fossils than at us.

Geddes MacGregor, my philosophy professor, deeply Scottish but, as he pointed out to me, of the Campbell clan, the natural enemy of my own MacDonalds, wore a green tweed suit every day and lectured at the ceiling. I had loved the early Greeks, especially Thales and Anaximander, but Boethius I remember as my downfall. Or maybe it was a clan problem. But I read the proofs of Geddes MacGregor's book called *Christian Doubt* for him, awed by the idea of a Presbyterian doubting something. We Episcopalians doubted a lot, no problem about that. And then there were the questions posed by my next philosophy professor, Milton Nahm, tubby and smart, with round glasses, whom I respected because he had put together the Greek anthology we were using, and I loved the idea that everything in it was a fragment. But I was never to be a success in philosophy:

Argue with Plato, Miss Rorison: where does he have it wrong?

I couldn't figure out where he did have it wrong, it seemed pretty good to me, better than anything I could say or write or think about caves or the light or anything else.

Why did you come to college, Miss Rorison?

asked Dr. Nahm. Why indeed?

But I kept cramming things in, as much as I could, three things at a time without reflecting on any of them, gulping down everything I could read and see and write. Time was never enough. like never having been able to give my beloved grandmother even half a day so she could teach me to bake one of her cakes. It all sped by, like everything else.

My roommate fixed my hems and waited up for me; Dr. MacGregor set me to reading yet more book proofs (despite our clan difference); my Spanish teacher set me to translating poetry; and some of my poems were published by the editor of the literary magazine, Joanna Semel. What delighted me about her was as much her total incapacity for swimming as her sparkling wit. I was in utter admiration, since, with her brain, she couldn't pass the swimming test necessary for graduation, which consisted of treading water for two minutes. I cannot fathom the usefulness of this skill for a Bryn Mawr graduate or anyone else, except in the oddest of circumstances. Nevertheless, we were all required to demonstrate it, and Joanna, who managed everything with aplomb, arranged to be supported from beneath by the frail tiny woman professor of Greek. Joanna proved, then and later, to have more significant talents than treading water, and if we all knew the underside of that particular swimming test, we never told. That was part of our code, in which I wholeheartedly believed, certainly more than in the college's honor code or in myself.

College was like that. Even as it rushed by, I felt paradoxically that it would never end. More time would suddenly be made for everyone, and none of us would have empty hands or heads.

By a piece of tremendous luck, my always best friend Sarah Bird arrived to live in the same hall. She would serve tea every afternoon, and a group of friends would gather. We would wish on everything: the first slice of lemon, the first day of every month. It was like wishing on the first star that everyone in the world would be happy, no one would be hungry, and my father would not drink too much. It seemed right to hope all this.

One day, a lighthearted and engaging speaker in horn-rimmed glasses—my favorite kind—had come to lecture us on the glories of the Sweet Briar Junior Year Abroad. The idea instantly captured me. You could spend all year in Paris and still get credit, as if you had stayed in Pennsylvania? Although I knew no French at all, I certainly wasn't going to let anything so basic as language stand in my way. The next day after the lecture, I suddenly gave up the German I had been learning in imitation of my mother to plunge into what we called baby French. I loved the idea of leaving college for a year, wanting to try something else, anything at all I might be offered. I was still waiting for something to happen. If I was somewhere else, it just might.

In France, things seemed more intense. We were sent to Tours to improve our accents: mine could certainly have done with some improvement, as could the language that the accent was meant to enhance. I think I drawled even in French. But no one ever corrected me.

Only two and a half inches of bath water were permitted, this postwar period being still a time of scarcity. I loved it all. My French family served *boudin,* blood pudding, usually black, but occasionally white. Monsieur sang songs of the revolution, and I was happy. I would take my bike out to the river and practice at the top of my lungs, as best I could, the words of what he sang, and go home to the everlasting and always comforting evening soup, the *potage du soir,* just as I did at home.

Later in Paris, the very different family I stayed with—a step up on the social scale, and far less easygoing—had a distinct melancholy about it. My

Polish and British roommates spoke in low tones at the table, as did the members of the family: a glum nurse always in black and a banker son, with the corners of his mouth perpetually turned down. I suspect he had it in for his mother for accepting money to take foreign boarders into her home. Over the painfully long coffee service after lunch, there was never a word spoken at all.

This was not the European volubility I had been led to expect through my reading. No wonder. Madame's husband had been murdered in the closet by the Germans, and there was no laughter, even when the overbred Persian cat climbed up the silk-covered walls. We had been warned never to bring home any German friend, never to discuss war or politics, for sensitivity ran high. Nor were we to wear yellow: did they claim it was the color for prostitutes? I didn't figure that one out, but listened and obeyed, of course.

At the Catholic Institute where I went to study philosophy, the discussions were centered around something I knew too little about:

> Father, excuse me please. I am not a Catholic, I don't know exactly what "our philosophy" is. Forgive me,

I found myself saying, surprised I could get up the nerve to do so. A square-jawed young man with a sweet intense face came up to talk to me about the pope's experience at Canossa. Either his horse knelt to the emperor's or the other way. I guess it was the other way, as would have been proper. I didn't care about the horse, only about looking at the young man, Jim. I loved his brown eyes, and the cleft in his chin made my year go far better.

Jim and I, with his other Fordham friends, Richard and Cornelius, would walk around the city all night and sleep in the day, missing our classes. On weekend trips to Vézelay or Azay-le-Rideau, we would spend the night in the fields, freezing and pure. I believed in France and all the friendships made there, never got over it, and never wanted to come home.

In fact, I had to come home two months early. I hated it. I hated the prospect of the whole next year. Mother insisted on my being a debutante, while I knew I'd never be graceful, charming, or anything else it seemed to require. I had, after all, been sent away to the country when I was in grammar school, to my grandmother's plantation, to learn how to be graceful. It had not taken.

I would have thought my grandmother would have stood up for me, finding such outmoded customs artificial. But that part of the South had her as well as me in its grip, and naturalness had no place there. Couldn't Grandmother stick up for me somehow? With all her spunk and energy, she was bound to understand: I kept thinking this. Apart from her dreadful opinions that one shouldn't appear smart, and that ladies are supposed to wear corsets or girdles, both of which I put down to her generation, she had always been on my side. I said my sister, Peg, hadn't had to do this, that it wasn't like me, that I didn't believe in it, and it was mortifying to have to borrow funds in order to finance it. I cried so much I had no more protest left, and went through with it.

> *Grandmother and I are going to pick out a dress for one of the events. She goes with me into the dressing room to help counsel me. I trust her; I always have. It is a bright blue dress I am trying on, and Mother has pointed out it will go with my eyes. I am skeptical, particularly since it is satin, loathsome stuff. I hate satin and all it represents. I look in the mirror—it looks all right, but too shiny. Then I look at the price tag: it costs far too much in my opinion.*

Lovely,

> *says Grandmother, smiling in her wonderful way, and pats my hip where the dress is clinging.*
>
> *To my astonishment and terror, I slap her hand away. I slap my grandmother's hand, which was only there from affection, my grandmother whom I love more than anyone.*
>
> *What is wrong with me? How can I tell her what I feel? My panic at not being me? Her own blue eyes I've inherited have a look of understanding in them. She has known what I feel. I have behaved abominably against the being I most respect, and she bears no grudge.*

I had to choose six escorts to take me around in turn, knowing perfectly well that they would rather have been elsewhere. I was certain I was going to trip coming down the stairs so very slowly, clutching the two dozen long white roses I strongly disliked. I was sure I was going to get killed driving up those chapel steps in one escort's car, with him reeling about at the wheel. Bobby de Rossett he was, a family friend and so not to be criticized. My smile kept going wrong, and what was the point? My cheeks were always going to be fat, and I was never going to have grace of any kind, it seemed. Too late to get it.

The day before Grandmother died, in a nursing home where everyone loved her, as everyone always had, she shared with the nurses the piece of watermelon Mother had brought her. I was already married and wished Grandmother had known I was about to have my first child: she longed for me to have one during all the years we didn't. I felt lost in the world without her. Nunny was there then to talk it over with and to make us custard. That day, we ate it hot from the oven, smooth in places and with raised brown parts, and my hand shook when I was supposed to add the nutmeg. Grandmother was the one I had loved the most.

Three

Together

NO MATTER HOW MUCH I would prefer not to remember, some grave things have to be reexamined if I am to retrace a journey really taken. What was it about Peter that appealed to me so instantly and held me so that I thought it would be for a lifetime? He was completely unlike anyone else I'd known; Perhaps I was smitten by otherness.

After graduation from Bryn Mawr, I tried to get a job at the Yale University Press, eager as I was to be in the same town as Bobby, the glamorous artist and pianist who had broken my piano's sounding board. This was before he had figured out that his destiny was with members of his gender, not mine. Incapable as I was of typing, my ambition fell flat. We had been urged at college not to learn to type, lest we end up doing just that, and now that I wanted to, clearly I could not learn in time. Roberta Yerkes, head of the Press, had tried to get me to type a paragraph on whales, blue ones, as I remember. I tried a dozen times, until she said with a wry smile: "Miss Rorison, there is a good university right around the corner." And there was.

So I ended up in Yale's French department. At one noisy party, I met Peter, a thin English student dressed more informally than anyone else there. His sleeves rolled up, his dark hair falling over his eyes, he was speaking to the others in impassioned tones about Kepler and his experiments. Someone ventured to tell me, when I asked about him, that he had come to Yale on an international fellowship to work on philosophy of science with Henry Margenau, a celebrated professor. When several of us walked back to my dorm, chance found Peter and me side by side. I imagined he would rather be with one of those long-haired maidens with bright eyes who had surrounded him at the party. I was always good at imagining, better than at some other things that might have proved more useful.

Shortly after that, in the dining hall, we found ourselves seated near each other, and began an argument about poetry. Here I felt myself on surer ground than on facts of any kind, philosophical, scientific, historic. Alas for my ground, he was surer than me there too, knowing reams of poetry by heart, and as passionate about it as I was. I had just begun to enjoy myself greatly, to the point of forgetting that he would probably rather be talking with someone else, when he excused himself and sauntered off to a Lubitch film, whistling under his breath.

The next week, a group of us were invited to a friend's house in the country and were to meet outside the Yale Co-op building. When I arrived late, in my flat shoes and college blazer, I felt immensely less sophisticated than the others. But my clothes seemed suited to playing croquet in the country, and I found Peter smiling at me. That day, he took a picture of me scowling over my croquet mallet at him, which he appeared to find very funny. I was scowling because this Britisher appeared to know nothing at all about proper manners and sacrificing himself to let the lady win. That interested me. It was as if a close relation between us had already been sealed. When we sang together around the piano, Peter was playing, sight-reading the score, breathing heavily. Everything he did, he did intensely: how could I not have fallen in love?

Coming home, me sitting on his bony lap, we played Botticelli in the car: you think of someone whose last name begins with a letter, say S. The other person then asks if you are, for example, a famous composer. If you cannot name a famous composer whose name begins with S, the asker gets to ask a direct yes-no question. I loved the game, but Peter was certainly making up the rules to suit himself, I thought. I found him arrogant, but accepted his suggestion that we meet at church the next day, since we had found we were both Anglicans, me lapsed, him taking instruction, for he had been part of another faith in England. I knew how those things went: I was used to making dates on Saturday night for an early morning Sunday meeting, and the next morning only I would appear. Indeed, after the service, instead of looking around for him, I fled back to my dormitory, overcome by my recurring shyness.

Two days later, he appeared at the bottom of my dormitory stairs, having looked for me, he said, in the library. Peering at him from the top step, with my just-washed hair in a turban, I was what my family would have called a sight. In the basement kitchen, I fixed him some Postum, that cereal beverage I liked for its muddy color and ambivalent taste. How did it happen? A few nights later, I found myself inviting him to visit me in the South, heard him accept, and removed the veal from the water I had thought you should boil it in. This was the first supper I had cooked for anyone in my life. Though the veal had, of course, no taste, he seemed not to notice. Or at least he didn't comment upon it.

We took endless walks in the country, through cemeteries and by streams; we picnicked by deserted houses and on beaches. Peter talked to me about science, Byzantine culture, and himself. He always felt equipped to deal not just with history and science and philosophy, but with explanations about them all. He could, in fact, classify and explain anything. Never did he seem to be at a loss for words or ideas. Still, there was about him something sad, hidden, not at ease.

His mother was of a strict, straitlaced, and evangelical sect called the Plymouth Brethren, to which she had converted his father. It was more severe as Peter recounted it to me than I could imagine, even through remembering Edmond Gosse's *Father and Sons,* the story of Gosse's own family, of the same belief. The Brethren were allowed no radio, no music other than religious, no books other than the Bible and its interpretations, no worldly anything, no voting, on and on. Women could not cut their hair; men had to wear hats; worship services abounded; and the testifying to and questioning of others was constant. Peter had broken away from the sect in coming to America to study philosophy, a topic outlawed to the children of Brethren, as were humanities in general. At home, he would have remained under the watchful eyes of both parents, constantly on the lookout for a slip into infidelity, heresy, sin.

You could slip into misdoings in many forms. You could misinterpret a verse in the Bible, or you could fail to bear witness. You had to testify to the Lord Jesus in any place and before anyone when you possibly could, including friends and strangers. Peter was forced to bear witness always, even when he was most embarrassed about it. His mother would put a Bible in his suitcase for the weekend he would be sent to spend with properly worshipping brethren. All of this struck a strangely discordant note considering his present cast of mind, his talkativeness and brilliance. He was more complex than my other friends, attractively, even seductively tormented as they were not. His background was far more peculiar than mine, even as his inner sadness corresponded to my own.

He would receive letters like sermons from overseas, in crabbed handwriting, with many layers of postscripts on the back. I would sometimes read the backs of these envelopes, intrigued with the intricacy of the whole system. It seemed written in code. And he would read aloud to me from these missives, that went something like this:

> My dear: have you thought of how Timothy 3:14 corresponds to Matthew 5:6? Let us consider this further.
>
> Have you borne witness lately, my child?
>
> Is the teaching bearing fruit? [Corinthians 6:15–20, especially verse 17].

Peter would grip the lunch table when the mail came. He was taking instruction to become an Anglican, like me, but not—I was sure—because of me. He was making such rapid progress and was so convincing a believer-to-be—Peter was seldom unconvincing—that he was queried as to whether he would care to become a priest.

I was attracted, as I see it now, by his private anguish. Perhaps, as many friends suggested to me later, I had felt the vocation to heal, to minister as my mother had, to those in need. Something must have drawn me to that inner pain, clearly, like a fate I didn't grasp. Much of Peter I was never to understand, including the elements I loved the most.

He was definitely not like the others I knew at Yale. There was the time we were playing baseball at a house party. Peter, having hit what looked like a home run, just smiled, remaining stock-still in place, wiping his brow with a white and blue checkered handkerchief. He never thought of running. Cricket was a different game. He was a substitute on Yale's cricket team, and to my everlasting pride, he one day wore my belt as his own. But this was certainly not cricket, and he was supposed to run.

Oh dear, he exclaimed to us, Am I supposed to be doing something?

I found this all engaging and refrained from asking the reaction of my friends. Peter did not yet know American rules for anything. Nor did he care to learn other rules than his own. He played games, from Botticelli to baseball, as if he were setting the pace and the laws, nonchalant and low-key glamorous. He had, as was clear, the best of both worlds, and I loved both of them in him. He was foreign, but he was to be my home.

His rather stilted language I thought of in the beginning as charmingly Old World; it had something of that biblical ring you heard in his family's letters. I loved looking at his gaunt cheeks under his mop of thick hair, loved his stories, his voice, his face. We would hold hands in the sentimental films we loved, feel ourselves involved in Graham Greene's dilemmas, his doomed couples. His *End of the Affair* seemed a protection against our own ever ending. We would argue over literature and life, over Diderot and Pascal, my once private passions, and Hopkins and Henry James, passions we shared. Peter would tell me how history occurred. I didn't argue as well as I gave in; he seemed to think this was just the way it should be. Of course: he knew and I just felt, wasn't that it? Wasn't that always to be it?

We would quarrel over nothing and make up, weep at parting until Peter had to drive around to get his eyes dry. So this was what our love was to be like. Did Peter keep thinking back to all the girls he'd known? I knew that he had loved others, figures of fantasy and real ones. No doubt many had been as attracted to him as I was. Had there not been Ariane in the Lake District and Isabella on the beach at Torquay?—I imagined her long hair streaming in the wind. Had there not been Philippa with the horses, and Daphne making tea somewhere on the downs? Why couldn't I just have been born English? Much simpler all around. I knew something about Europe, but as he enjoyed pointing out to me and others, including my friends, I expressed myself timidly even in what I knew. Especially in what I knew, southern style.

Peter had wanted to try the New World, give it a fling, see how it compared. It was all right, and he stayed here. Would I wait if he went off on a weather ship for a year, as he had always longed to? He thought not, and I thought not either. So it had had to be the way it was.

I will do your mopping and cleaning for you,

I heard myself saying one day. I was thinking then that I would never long for a career. How could that have been? My friends knew I did; Peter knew I did; how could I not have known?

We were both finishing our theses, his a dense five hundred pages of philosophy of science, and mine, a mere ninety-six pages on what I called the poetics of possibility, comparing the surrealist writer André Breton and the philosopher Gaston Bachelard. I had become interested in precisely what was thought to be absurd, irrational, unreadable. Due perhaps to my own arrogance, I wanted to make sense of what might have been thought devoid of interest, or indeed sense.

Easy stuff,

said Peter with a quiet smile, about my thesis. Ah, perhaps it was. I would always rather concur than confront. If it was all that obvious, I was unlikely to find anyone to publish it, but I scarcely cared. I was, after all, in love with Peter. What did the rest matter?

We went down to North Carolina to see my family. I hadn't decided to tell them I was finally in love, but presumed it was obvious. It was warm enough to walk along the deserted beach for hours, under a smudgy sky.

It undoes in the back,

I said of my bra to Peter.

How nice, he said.

Later, we came home to the sound of Mother's pacing steps. But still there was a cake set out on a good plate. She was a lady of manners.

He doesn't have all his cards on the table,

said my father, poker player that he was, of this man I loved. And kept looking at his newspaper.

Back at Yale, Peter proposed to me in a bargain diner on Chapel Street, over the baked apple and pallid coffee. In a Toddle House the next week, I accepted. My grandmother, I told him, had taught me not to hesitate about what is worth doing. Waiting for the pecan waffle, I phoned my father, who reserved judgment. His first statement on the topic did not come until some weeks later, when the *New York Times* could fit our notice into their pictures and announced engagements. When he said yes, I wondered if he had forgotten his feeling that Peter was hiding something. I could not bring myself to ask, and knew he would not have answered.

We were to be married at Yale, rather than in my native South, so that Peter would not feel overcome by southern ceremony and customs. Before the wedding rehearsal one evening, I was suddenly overcome with panic. There were gathered all the bridesmaids and groomsmen and my family and our friends, all presumably rejoicing, and I panicked. At my dormitory, Bobby, the original reason I had come to New Haven, was playing the piano. A Beethoven sonata, no. 110, my favorite. Marriage was supposed to be making me happy. Suddenly I found myself sobbing in his arms, as startled as he was. Why did he have to be gay? Couldn't we have made a better life than I would have with Peter? I could not go on with this, had no wish to marry a foreigner, disliked the idea of marriage anyway, found it all too rapid. But now I had to go rehearse to prepare for the act that I didn't want to commit.

The ceremony was held in the tiny Dwight Chapel, behind the larger Battell Chapel, where Bobby sang in the choir on Sundays, gorgeous in his blue robe. At least in New Haven, Peter had his friends for our marriage. Given their beliefs and their budget, there was no way his family would or could have come over for the ceremony. I wore Mother's and Grandmother's wedding dress, with its ivory Alençon lace train sweeping down the narrow aisle. My father, one leg shorter than the other, did not limp at all—what that must have cost in pain, I can only imagine. Never had I seen him walk without limping.

I have no idea what went on in the actual service, except for one of the responses, in which I had refused to use the traditional "obey." As it was an option now, I had substituted for it the term "cherish," the same one the groom uses. I felt vaguely nervous at my substitution, at the very moment of pronouncing it. Something about changing a tradition.

Most of the time, my mind was on whether we were supposed to kiss at the altar, and whether I would trip over the long train going back out. My sister, Peg, was the dame of honor, Sarah Bird, the maid of honor, and I think we were all holding the blue cornflowers I loved. In any case, the beauties of the marriage service escaped me totally.

It was pouring outside, which I took as a sign of future doom. At the reception in the Hall of Graduate Studies, full of Greek and Latin toasts with New England ladies of intellectual mein in long dresses and my southern family bedecked in gracious smiles, a family loving cup was passed around, the same one used for all the weddings in our large Anglo-American family, the Lippitts and the Gages. This was supposed to guarantee happiness.

I had neglected to explain American customs to my husband. While our friends stood by the car with their rice to throw at us and songs to sing on our departure, Peter calmly showered as they all waited. His notions seemed often to have no connection with the outside world. Nor did mine—we made an odd match, but a remarkably good one, as long as it lasted.

We went to call on Mrs. Knight, the old lady Peter had chauffeured around New Haven for years. And then went on somewhere else.

Peter and I, and the Egg

Before we went down to the college in Wilmington, for Peter's summer job, we had a week's honeymoon, and for it, a choice. A tiny cottage on Cape Cod lent by one family friend or a cabin lent by another, at the top of Grandfather Mountain in North Carolina, closed to the public after sunset. Having chosen the latter, we arrived and saw just how tiny tiny was. What struck me most was the double-decker bed, scarcely suitable for togetherness.

Yet what should perhaps have struck me more was Peter's general demeanor. Or mine; or ours together. It was apparent we had a great deal to work out. In the morning, for example. He took, he in fact required, eggs for breakfast. From my experience with English bed-and-breakfasts and inexpensive hotels, I already knew most English people had an egg, a pair of tepid grayish sausages, a dissolved tomato, and toast deliberately set to cool in a silvered toast rack. I had, however, failed to imagine what this would mean in daily living, as act or symbol.

Soft-boiled,

said Peter.

Please. Three minutes. Thank you. Let's not worry about the toast.

It was not the toast I was worrying about, but it was surely something in his tone, or the air. I found a saucepan, put some water in it to boil, lowered the egg into the said water with a teaspoon as one of my housemates, Marie Boroff—specialist of, among other texts, *Gawain and the Green Knight*—had showed me at graduate school. We surrealists had been far less practical. I timed three minutes, broke the shell, put the unappealing yellow thing in a cup, and handed it to Peter, who was happily ensconced in something by Whitehead. He took the cup with one hand and took up his spoon in the other. And addressed me, smiling vaguely at the page:

Darling, he said, how nice.

I recognized the same tone he had used to express his happiness that my bra undid in the back. That was good. Then he cracked the egg and looked at it, suddenly not good at all:

Mary Ann.

he said quietly, holding in his temper with evident strain.

This is not a three-minute egg. What is this anyway?

I could find nothing to say. My father on my fatness; my silence.

I am so sorry, darling, said Peter. Could you fix me a proper one, please? Thanks so much, do you mind awfully?

He returned to his reading. I really do not know how to say what happened in me then. I saw a red light exploding or several of them. Irrational isn't the word for it. I picked up the cup and threw it to the floor, where it shattered with a satisfying clatter.

Peter, to do him justice, was quite courteous about it, gentlemanly in fact. He spent hours driving me from store to store to find a matching cup to replace what my temper had undone. Never questioned me about my anger, never raised his voice. I am even now at a loss to explain what happened in me, but it was to repeat itself. Usually in combination with Peter.

Years later, when we were at the University of Kansas in the 1960s, I was teaching French literature, and Peter—who had by this time become distinctly more relaxed, almost American in temperament and style—was chairing the philosophy department. One day, he suggested we ask his colleagues over. Perfectly normal, I knew, but strangely and suddenly I was taken by the same irrational feeling as all those years before, on our honeymoon. Having prepared the neatly cut sandwiches and potato chips and little dips, all the things we thought necessary for the occasion, I felt something rush over me. I seized the coffeepot and, with all of the guests watching in horror, carefully poured the steaming contents over everything: the chips, the dips, the sandwiches. Then I went to our bedroom. No one said a word, including Peter. I wanted to feel sorry, but didn't.

Once in our bedroom, I did not know how to come out. Should I apologize in front of all of them? Leave it to fate? strictly speaking, to Peter, the way I usually did? I cannot now remember how it ended, except that I think there was no reprimand, or questioning, except of myself by me.

What could have been going on in me, in all this anger? Inherited from my father and only showing itself after all this time? Unanswerable. It is all a blur. But it is part of my story, perhaps not the least significant part.

EARLY ON

We had, nevertheless, what can only be described as a glorious early marriage, physically, emotionally, intellectually. We did all sorts of things together, and Peter never seemed bored. Either with me or my whims: I began to relax and believe I could be loved. We walked in all kinds of weather, holding hands in our raincoats or our shorts, took trips long and less long, discussed what we were reading and teaching, and how our classes were going, had long chats over tea, and made cookies together. Peter would play the piano and I would turn the pages. He would lecture me on this and that and I would listen. As for the soft-boiled eggs, he learned to prepare them. It felt right.

That summer in Wilmington, when Peter was teaching philosophy at Wilmington College, we lived in a backroom at my grandmother's, by her studio. I would go in there in the early morning and marvel at what she did and loved. Peter would teach in the mornings, and in the afternoons we would join other couples for picnics and outings—it felt like a continuation of the honeymoon, as did many of the years after that summer. I think it was about rhythms: we did the same thing at the same time, without considering how unusual that was.

Yes, that was it: our personal rhythms matched in everything that mattered—at work as at play. As if by some miracle, we always got bored at the same time when we were working in libraries, and would get up for coffee, wherever we were, to go out together. In the years after Wilmington, when I had realized I needed to work, do research, and write, we were working together at the Bibliothèque Nationale in Paris, side by side under the little green lights in the old library that so many of us loved. We would rise as one and go to the neighboring café for an *express,* and then return, eager to get back to our work. Same thing at the Reading Room in the British Library—again, the old one, under its dome, where Karl Marx and Virginia Woolf and so many others had read and thought—where we would go down to the tearoom at the same moment. No discussion needed. While that may not seem so important, to me it betokened some deep communion of mind and soul. And so it was. You could tell, or at least we could. We had the same stride, outside and in. We would take the same turn at the corner, settle at the bar, comfortable in each other's company. We would go around museums at our separate pace, always ending up in the same spot at the same moment, always eager to take each other back around to see our favorite things. Peter would grin, the tiny space between his front teeth showing.

This was true for all the first years of our marriage. I think now that we were very fortunate to have them.

READING ALOUD

Peter liked to read aloud, at length, from books poetic and historical, old and new, in several languages. I enjoyed it too, yet when I was to read to him, I turned out not to be an elegant reader. Whereas I had done some acting at school and some declamation under my mother's tutelage, I proved to be next to tongue-tied in this situation. Some words I would trip over, others I would swallow, stumbling and mumbling. I *knew better.* Why was I incapable next to him, whom I loved? It seemed to make no sense. We were continually colliding over this kind of thing, my uncertainties and his self-possession running straight into each other. But it wasn't something we could discuss.

I wasn't good at discussing. I was not just somewhere else often in geography, but also in spirit; I could not deal with difficult things, and our marriage was to become one of these.

In the 1960s, first at Michigan State and then at the University of Kansas, we would use the opposite ends of a very long teak table, occupying the center of our room. In the center, we would leave a space for meals, to save clearing our things away. After meals, we would take off the dishes, clean everything up, and move to opposite ends across the great divide in the middle. Biting my nails in distracted concentration on some text I was reading or writing—things I would never, could never give up, forget my having wanted to—I would catch Peter's eyes upon me. They were what my mother would have called keen. I hated their keenness. Peter did not bite his nails, did not have trouble concentrating. He simply did whatever task he had assigned himself, beginning to end, and went on to the next one. Smart, determined, self-assured: it was scary.

Never, I think, had Peter ever read a book from the ending backward, the way I do when I want to know whether it is worth spending time on. I could always recognize John Updike, for instance, by the ends of his stories, or Mavis Gallant, or a number of others. I *liked* reading ends first. To Peter this was incomprehensible. Worse, it was distasteful.

Last thing at night, Peter would make Horlick's malted milk for both of us. He would carefully heat the milk, measure out two tablespoons of the powder into each cup, spoon a little of the heated milk ("not boiled, do you see, Mary Ann?") onto the powder, stir it exactly thirty seconds, pour the rest of the milk over the paste, and stir again. ("See, this is the way you do it.") Nary a drop spilled, and he never made too much. Surely this was supposed to feel like security: Peter, Horlick's, and a job: first as a librarian in Michigan, then a teacher in Kansas, always a faculty wife. Why did I continually feel that something was missing?

As for Peter's rather formal way of speaking and being, I told myself I didn't mind. It felt like acting. After all, I had been trying out in private, for years, the personalities of the people I was writing on or lecturing about. Like a child dressing up. I put on Scottish and Slavic accents, French and German, anything but my own. Wanting to look like an artist, I draped myself in droopy clothes to write, like Virginia Woolf, with steel-rimmed glasses. I even tried out places. For Woolf, thanks to Sarah Bird who was living there for a while, we stayed at Monk's House in Rodmell. For John Ruskin—because of whom I first loved Turner—we stayed at Brantwood in the Lake District one summer; we took turns sitting in his great stone chair along his path. We walked in his woods, climbed the Old Man of Coniston, his favorite hill. Later, I practiced hitting myself on the forehead, like Wittgenstein, huddling up in a chair with mittens on like Glenn Gould, minus piano. I could always put back on my southern drawl, that I had never really lost, even living with that so-British tone Peter exuded: "Your broken dialect," as one student said to him. He would often recount that.

Peter was at first amused by my fuzzy relation to the world: inside my imaginings, you didn't have to deal with facts. He had had to deal with those, and a lot more: the war, the modest earnings of his father, the strict religious constraints of the Plymouth Brethren. Heavier than anything, he was always to feel doomed and damned for leaving the family, their church, and his country.

I am a rotter,

he would say, from the beginning, and then later.

But for a while we made a good team: when we visited my family in North Carolina, he'd spend hours with Peg, who was as serious as I was chaotic and flippety. After being a researcher for *Time* magazine, she had taught school, and then had her own program, *Getting the Message,* on New York's Channel 13, teaching teachers how to teach difficult students. She was now developing a similar program, *Getting the Word,* for a television station in Columbia, South Carolina, and going to Wilmington on weekends to be with the family. She would bring all sorts of questions for Peter, when we went home on vacation. They got along.

Peter enjoyed driving our old Plymouth, wherever we were. When we had come home to Wilmington for vacation, he would drive about very slowly with me and my always best friend Sarah Bird, one on each fender, exploring woods and beaches until we would stop for our picnic. That was when there were still forests near my hometown—Piney Woods, they were called—we would go for a gentle ride on the car bumpers, along the uneven paths and little-frequented roads. There was something magical about it. Then we'd spread out our picnic on some overturned log in the spatterings of sunlight, our feet prickled by the orange-colored pine straw making a floor beneath us.

That was in America. In England in the summers, we didn't see Peter's parents very often, for everyone felt uncomfortable, not just me. I always felt left out of everything: English culture, school gossip, religious fervor, and quite especially the family memories of their expeditions up hills and over to neighboring brethren for weekends or for tea. I wasn't as good with his younger sister as he was with my beloved Peg or with Sarah Bird, and the others were too religious for him to see. His overpowering mother, with her hair in a strict steel-gray bun, was much harsher than his rather gentle father with his thin face and glasses. She didn't take to me, blaming me for Peter's departure from the fold and thinking Americans somewhat beyond the pale. She would stand on the step above and query me:

> I expect your father has a car, doesn't he?
> Yes,

I would say, and then dwell on the excuse part:

> but he's lame, and he has to get to work.
> Is that a party dress you are wearing?
> No, ma'am, it's polyester so it doesn't wrinkle.

It was a sickly green, with a button-down collar. Peter was wearing a seersucker suit—both these items of clothing were desperately wrong in the chill and gray of Southall, near London. And Peter's mother was not about to let me forget it.

> I expect you have lots of dresses, don't you, dear? I have very few.

And so on. There were no correct answers. Her father had been a railroad signalman, and mine, a southern banker. Plainly, and perhaps rightly, she didn't trust me any more than my father did Peter.

> Peter, my dear, you pronounce things so strangely now. Listen to you, you say bud-duh for butter. And that's not all . . .

No, it wasn't all by any means. It was easier just to hope my family could somehow make up for his own. In his, things were confused and embittered.

As they were often, it seemed to me, in his mind. Southern entanglements seemed almost mild alongside these.

I always wanted us to have the same nationality, and to that end, during the Vietnam War, I was to take out British citizenship, thinking this would give him a family at home. I swore fidelity to the queen on a white Bible covered in cellophane, and the names of the children were inscribed therein: they could eventually have double citizenship, as I do. "Lots of new subjects for the Queen," said the official.

A Big Chill

Perhaps our history could have been predicted from our pasts, perhaps not. Right after our marriage in 1962, at Michigan State University in East Lansing, we finally found two jobs. Peter was hired as an instructor, and I as a faculty wife. That is to say, I was given the post of assistant reference librarian for interlibrary loans. Forget my training, forget my longings, forget how basically *driven* I am: this job meant wrapping books for mailing and answering a question or two. My fault: I remembered saying how I would be content with mopping and ironing. But it was true, alas: I wanted to write, wanted to finish my graduate degree. At any rate, in Michigan, the intellectual life was not what you would call ideal, nor was the practical one very comfortable.

We lived all winter in a summer cottage by a lake. The chill was intense, and lasting. The bathtub was green canvas, purchased from a Sears catalog, which is what we could afford: after each use, we had to bring it downstairs and dump it out upon the lawn. The fish insisted on dying in the lake and floating to the top. This was not the way I had imagined the setting of our marriage. Peter found much to correct in my behavior and housekeeping, and I would lose my temper at him. So he always won.

I think it was the tub that got to me most. Not the cold in East Lansing, not the way the damp made everything feel moldy, but the tub and its care. Now Peter was not brought up to take his baths in a canvas tub. Actually, I was not either, even if I am Amurrican. I would rush to empty out the tub: it would be heavy coming down the stairs, and occasionally I would spill a good bit on the way. Hated it.

It did not perturb Peter. Unperturbed—he would remain always unperturbed—Peter would move with great precision toward the tub. Having finished the chapter he was reading or writing first, he would take this chore upon himself, with a small smile and total equanimity. That he always had, and I, rarely. I had ups and downs of enthusiasm, but equanimity I was not graced with. Everything seemed on the same level for Peter, who actually made me a design about our difference: my pattern wavered drastically, and his line was smooth.

Not bad,

he would say of some piece of writing or cooking. As for the derogatory remarks, they were similarly low key. Peter was a very muted man. I wanted to mute myself.

I would try to enthuse less over small things. Enthusiasm is definitely in my nature, and I would have to struggle against it here, as I did when I was little. In Michigan, however, by the frozen lake, my ongoing struggle was generally satisfactory, as it was at my job. My boss sniffled all the time in the reference section of the library and left little wads of used Kleenex around; I continued to mail out books on interlibrary loan. At lunch, I would read. The rest of the time, I would staple things together and pack books. I would sometimes be allowed to look things up, if the reference librarian could not figure out where to do this, which occurred with a certain frequency.

So much I never learned: like the relationship between chlorophyll and why leaves turn brown—is there one? I could never understand the science part of newspapers, let alone the games. A user had only to ask something like:

In what year did the Cardinals . . . or the Dodgers . . . or Billie Jean King . . .

and my mind would go completely blank.

As for the teaching I had thought I had been preparing myself to do at Yale, it was pointed out to me that I had only a master's degree and, on top of that, from an eastern institution. In those places, said the head of the foreign language department, "they teach differently." There was, he continued, "a different clientele" here in the Midwest, so how could I have expected a teaching job? I had, though. Stanley, one of Peter's colleagues, pointed out helpfully that perhaps I could serve as an assistant to Peter for his research.

You seem to have a brain,

he said with a little smile.

I am greatly relieved,

I was about to say, but took a breath, as Mother had taught me to, and said nothing. How could I be so sarcastic, when he had meant well? Fuming inside, I thanked Stanley, who had his hand on my arm. Learn gratitude, Mary Ann, in a hurry.

Books frequently disappeared from the library. There was no one to check on this at the door. Nor did anyone seem to find it humorous that the chapter on ethics was razored out from *Hastings' Encyclopedia.* I found this ironic, as I did the fact that there were so many theses written about eggs: it was, after all, a state university, but the eggs got to me. My past, I suppose. Our past, Peter's and mine.

I read avidly at lunch and began to hatch the scheme of writing for myself someday. A novel about southern living, that is what I would most like to do, and "I seemed to have a brain," after all. I presumed that, even married to an Englishman, even an ex–Plymouth Brother from Southall, I would still count as southern, although upon occasion, I was finding it hard to count as anything at all.

What with the green canvas bathtub and our lakeside living, Peter and I were thrown much into each other's company. Yet coming from such different backgrounds, our views on entertaining were bound to differ somewhat, as did our views on many things. My idea of making dinner was something like watercress soup and roast chicken, salad, and almond cake with raspberries. But I wanted to impress Peter, so I planned more grandly.

These were the days when we were still going to an Anglican church. One evening, we were having the minister and his wife over for dinner. I always checked with Peter before preparing anything. I am not now sure exactly why I did this: I must have heard my mother doing so with her husband. In any case, I thought Peter expected it.

Ah, I think I'll make sorrel soup, what do you think?

Peter is plunged in his book. I should be in mine. I look up *soupe à l'oseille*, in Elizabeth David.

But where exactly do you get sorrel around here, in Michigan, by the lake? Can I make a proper *vitello tonnato?* Does our veal here have any taste? Do I want to add something from Jane Grigson's *Mushroom Feast?* Do I cook the main course and then the soufflé, or can I prepare the basic part of the soufflé while I am going along? Do we have any Grand Marnier? I am using Bee Nilson's *Desserts.* I am feeling used.

My mind is not on *vitello tonnato.* It is on a lecture I am supposed to give so the people at the university can see I know how to teach, say, a course on modern French writers if there just happened to be a need. Peter could of course do it all, but then, he *is* Peter. I look in at him. He has both feet up in his Cordovan loafers from Clark's (my father's style, but with tassels), darkish brown socks (knee-high), beige whipcord trousers, and an open-necked olive green shirt with a foulard from Liberty's. His horn-rimmed glasses are sitting slightly forward on his nose. My jeans are torn at the knee; my hair is hanging limp with my mind likewise.

Now it has happened. Forget dinner for the moment. My index cards for my upcoming lecture have just spilled all over the floor. The lecture is supposed to be witty and light. "Surrealism and the Shakes," I have called it. I have another: "Fearing Foucault," but it doesn't have the same zip. There on the floor are hundreds of cards, unnumbered (of course), and scattered every which way. I am chaos.

One cold day in the unheated cottage by the Michigan lake, in a fit of jealousy, I grab the scissors from the desk. I slash my favorite picture of Peter as a teenager, with that mop of hair I love, right across the middle. Another day—or is it the same one? my rage clouds every such picture, even in retrospect—I see myself chasing him with a knife around the yard beside the lake with the dying and redolent fish, out of a jealous temper. Ridiculous there in full daylight, panicked at the possibility of really hurting this man I adore. I am clearly crazy at ten in the morning in my nightgown with a kitchen knife, like some comic movie.

When we moved to the University of Kansas in 1963—"flat lands make flat minds," said our friends at Michigan State—we found a far more congenial atmosphere. I was allowed to work at the university press while getting my doctorate in romance languages and teaching. At the press, however, my dreams of editorial acumen remained unfulfilled. Each stylistic alteration I dared had to be checked with the authors, who all seemed given to flowery phrasing, the sort of fresh-winds-blowing-in-from-England style. I was in fact employed for what was thought to be my skill with commas.

And yet, I was never sure of any skill. Taking my comprehensive exams, I must have responded badly on at least one part. My adviser came to say, in front of an office full of my colleagues, how "disappointed" they all were in me. Unable to stop shaking, tears pouring down my face, I conferred with Peter.

I have let them down.
Oh, my dear, I am so sorry.

He really seemed to be.

How did you do that?

I explained, and Peter held me gently.

Well, perhaps you should consult with your chairman tomorrow. Go in first thing, why don't you? You'll feel better.

So I went to speak with J. Neale Carman, a specialist in medieval literature, the next day. His was the sort of mind that exulted in details: we had had to learn exactly five hundred words in Old French each week, no more, no less. Between uncontrollable sobs, I expressed my dismay that I had "let them all down." This was what you least wanted to do in the South, "let someone down." Dr. Carman was startled by the expression and protested:

Not at all, he said. You have it wrong.

Whichever way, I had it wrong: I often felt that. Either I was stubbornly persuaded I was right or afraid I was not up to what was expected. This pattern continued, familiar to many faculty wives: I always felt at fault.

I had really hated that time in Michigan and blamed perhaps too much upon it. How could I not have hated the sight and smell of those fish dying in the lake, and the imbalance in our jobs? I had felt unvalued and under-used, as well as unappreciated by others, and began to take their opinion for my own. Maybe after all, I should just be doing someone else's research, incapable of doing anything on my own. And maybe that would never change. Did Peter value my potential work, as my father had not? What could I write that wouldn't be desultory, vacuous? that would be more like philosophy? I had after all begun as a philosophy major, but who would know it now? Whereas on his side, Peter taught both philosophy and sci-ence, the latter about real facts, or so he said. We in literature felt less sure of facts and were supposed to spend our time questioning truth.

What was certain in this marriage was that his work was always to be given the importance it deserved. I sometimes wanted to question his judg-ment: philosophers did serious work, particularly concerning science and history, while literary types did pleasant unsubstantial essays, entertaining writing, or admittedly useful translations, always coming in second, of course, to the writings they served. Were the essays I had begun to publish unreservedly pleasant? They were developing, in any case, an edge they had not had before.

Peter had to teach courses in science and the history of thought seventeen hours a week. In one class, he was fond of showing the freshman girls how to prick their fingers to find their blood type, and in the other, teaching them how to "put their own thoughts in the light of Thought" or something like that. They seemed to find his help on such projects enormously enlightening. It certainly took a lot of time. I never somehow felt in the mood to do a lot of helpful research about that. Or in fact anything else. A rough year.

I have designs on your husband,

a dishy blonde in Peter's freshman science class said to me, and indeed I believed it: who wouldn't? I did too, after all. Surely no one could not be filled with the admiration for him that I was. Maybe that is what brought on the admiration of others, I found myself accusing myself.

Peter, a student is on the phone for you.
Fine, thank you, I'll take it in my study.

And then:

Mary Ann, I must leave for a few minutes.

Peter pointed out, gravely and rapidly, with his coat on, that the student was actually threatening to commit suicide unless he arrived instantly. Was I right, or insanely on the wrong track? I heard myself protesting:

Peter, don't you understand? They just want to get you out there. Darling, professors have duties to their successors in the field, which we should take seriously. I will be back before long.

and then, tenderly:

You look a bit frazzled: why not have a tiny nap?

Frazzled, yes, I was that. Even frenzied, with wondering continually about what was going on "historically," from initiator to successor "in the field." Frenzied. Perhaps crazy.

We are in a shopping mall in Kansas City. At some remark of Peter's that sounds utterly heartless to me, I rip off my blouse in fury. This pent-up anger recurring from childhood. It feels like slapping my grandmother so long ago, like pouring the coffee over the food for Peter's colleagues: why?

Why did I have all this anger in me, and why couldn't I, knowing it, help it? Peter was not to forget any of these scenes easily, perhaps ever. There were such scenes in Kansas, as there had been in Michigan, and as there were to be everywhere.

These were, all of them, rough years.

LATER

We moved, after our years in Kansas, to New York, Peter for a job at a funding corporation, me for a job at Barnard, part-time, but at least I could teach literature, as I had always longed to. Perhaps things would work out. I would have no recurrence of my fits of anger. I would be a normal grown-up with a grown-up job.

I am being offered a job at Barnard. My father says he greatly hopes "you are not taking money for it." I wonder how he thinks marriages survive on

one professorial salary these days? I am also having a book published, on
surrealism, based on my thesis, "A Poetics of Possibility." Excited, I phone
my parents. My mother suggests I write the publishers a thank-you note. It
is so good of them. My father wants to know how much I am being paid.

At Barnard, I continued to worry. My French was more enthusiastic than
perfect. They were all calm and elegant, my colleagues, it seems to me. At
ease, comfortable with each other, carefully dressed, and not a mistake in
French among them. I felt I was there on sufferance.

The department meetings take place in the deanery, with faculty members
offering in turn to bring the wine. When I think it is my turn, I am told
there is enough wine for the rest of the year. I bring marzipan candy. "How
nice," say my colleagues, each smiling graciously and sincerely.

At a small dinner with a few officials from Peter's Carnegie Corporation,
the vice president offers to try to find me a job in New York. Nothing, he
says, is too good for his employees' wives. I manage to stammer out that I
have one, but thank him as best I can. He is noticeably surprised and ex-
presses his delight with my good fortune.

Gracious me,

he says. I am delighted with my good fortune too, but concerned that it may
not last. I may be found out. Particularly in my forgetfulness about which
nouns are feminine and which masculine. This forces me to use a great many
circumlocutions, like *une espèce de*—that way, the noun's gender doesn't matter. Yet I was beginning to feel, even at women's colleges, that my own gender
did very much matter.

Time went on: we returned for a semester to Kansas, where Peter was offered
a prestigious teaching post and a large house with a piano. The foundation
let him go. I gave up my job at Barnard with regret, for LeRoy Breunig, the
gentle chairman and expert on Apollinaire and cubism, of whom I was very
fond, told me I would have been kept on. Our timing, he said, was bad. I
said how sorry I was. I was more than sorry, for I would have liked to stay.

When we returned to New York, I was pregnant. I lost my job at Hunter
College over this. My mother pointed out how right this was and suggested

I would not want my students to see me with a big tummy. She reminded me that when she was having Peg, she had not even gone up the church aisle to take communion.

When the baby had come, I got my job back, but in greatly reduced form and salary, for evening classes. Through our philosopher friend Richard Rorty, whose aunt was the president of Sarah Lawrence, I was offered a job there in the day, replacing Louise Bégué, who had a broken hip. I remained teaching at Hunter College at night. Always afraid of missing the train, I found the commute out to Sarah Lawrence in Bronxville mentally as well as physically tiring. I continued nursing Hilary, my baby daughter, of course, and only substituted the formula for the times I absolutely could not be there.

The babysitter was stern with me: "Baby hongry," she would say. "Baby hongry." Yes, baby was, and her mother, me, was exhausted with it all.

At that time the night course at Hunter College consisted of fifty beginning students who had worked all day, like me. Their heads would droop on their shoulders, but they all kept on. I was impressed, if exhausted. In the day, at Sarah Lawrence, my students were asked, by other students, "why they had chosen to study with a woman." Just as it was at Barnard, so it was at Sarah Lawrence. It was bad enough not to speak classically perfect French and not to have classically perfect features; it was worse, I felt, not to be a tall and elegant male, whose wife would pick him up at the train. Or to be able to stride down from the Bronxville train to the college, taking no time at all, like Frank Randall, a fellow teacher. I couldn't stride, never could.

Having to nurse the baby, wanting to write, and trying to overcome the feeling that I had, somehow, lost Peter's love, I almost succumbed to despair. My optimism and even my habitual enthusiasm ebbed. Things grew harder. I would teach; I would write; I would nurse my daughter; and I would spend the middle of every night reading. But I would not let on how hard I found it. Stubborn, and probably stupid.

For the Bryn Mawr alumnae magazine, I was asked to write up my experience of career and marriage. I tried to focus on what had really been going on in Michigan with the strain and the bathtub; then in Kansas, with my getting things wrong and Peter always getting them right; and finally in New York, where I kept hoping it would feel different. Whereas it had seemed to me in our preceding situations that life would be like that as long as it lasted, here it had a chance to change. I wanted to write a piece that would convince me, and others, that it would work. That you could commute, combine careers and family, and remain yourselves, together. I thought it sounded truthful and optimistic; later, a few perceptive readers told me how it sounded just the opposite. It was called, in a tone of hope, "A Double Allegiance," and I continued to hope. I felt that as a genuine possibility. But I did notice that every time someone would phone to offer me a job, it would be just when my baby was throwing a temper tantrum, or heading on all fours toward a bag of carpet tacks. Perhaps indeed I would not be able to write, read, or think any longer. I was not managing things well, Peter would have suggested, never saying it outright.

Perhaps indeed we had waited too long to have children. I had to write at night, to work in the day, to nurse my baby in between. When, at Sarah Lawrence, I'd have to rush back to the train, while all the leisurely gentlemen teachers were picked up by their smiling wives, I was angry at myself for not being able to drive because I tend to go to sleep at the wheel. "The road just doesn't keep her interest," the driving instructor explained to Peter. Peter would be his usual charming and efficient self, whereas I would enact my chaos, would throw up all over my students' papers when I was pregnant once more, and Peter would kindly be driving me up to Lehman in the Bronx where I was teaching now at night.

I was sure it would always be this way: me chaotic, him self-assured. He would write pieces that included me, poems and essays. I wrote that our marriage was worth what it took for what it gave, and called it a union of wit and love.

THOSE YEARS

The things I remember from the early years of our marriage all run together. I finally accepted a full-time position at Hunter College and hung on to it. It became available through an accident, a resignation, and a kind secretary, Elsie Fugett, whom I had contacted every two days to see if there might be something I could teach. My heart was pounding as I entered the chairman's office as I had before, for the part-time job. Once again, Emilio González, a gentleman in the Spanish style, but strongly aware of hierarchy, neither stood up nor looked up.

We may have a grammar class for you; nothing in literature, don't expect that.

I didn't, yet longed for it anyway. But I'd teach anything, gratefully. Again, as before, I was assigned to many students who wanted to begin to learn the language. Again, they came late at night after their work, hunched over their books, some smiling, a few sleeping.

I was able to get along with Professor Gonzalez by talking about Central Park. He came to work every day through the Rambles, that walk so inviting for bird lovers (which he was) and for those looking for sexual encounters (which he wasn't).

Eventually, I did get a literature course, and then more of them. My colleagues were delightful and friendly, and I began to feel at ease. Peter, who had finished up at the Carnegie Corporation ("Perhaps the academy," said the president of the corporation, who had hired him) was invited to chair the philosophy department at Hunter College, as a full professor. We began to act as a professorial couple. I wrote my articles and books, plunged into everything with the enthusiasm I thought I had lost, began to direct doctoral dissertations at the Graduate School of CUNY, taught my fifteen hours a week, cooked for my family, played with our children, and tried to hold things together. Most of all, I tried to hold us together. It felt possible then.

CABANON IN THE VAUCLUSE

After a joint sabbatical in 1972–73, in Paris, we decided to keep our sheets and the pepper mill we had acquired, and find somewhere to spend our summers in France. First, we tried L'Ile de Ré, which at that time had no bridge over from La Rochelle, and had excellent white wine and oysters. We found a place, made a down payment, and then I looked at a map. We were not in Provence, but on the wrong side of the country. My fault again. For during the sabbatical year, I had met the poet René Char, whom I had begun to translate and write about, and near whom we would all have liked to live, especially me.

So we lost our down payment on the Ile de Ré, and found, by some miracle, one night in Cassis, an ad in *Le Provençal* ("cabanon à aménager:

oliviers, cerisiers, amandiers, eau de source") . . . and succumbed, all of us happy. But there remains one great truth: to do anything well, you must already have done it. Thus, to buy anything here, it takes the practice you only get by buying—next time we buy a cabanon, I will know better how to do it. We, for we did this as a family, did not know how, until afterward. Briefly, it goes something like this: you spend two or three afternoons around a pastis, you and the agent, and size each other up. I take lots of water in my pastis; Peter takes a medium amount; and the agent took almost none—we were about to be a soft touch. What you lament in these long afternoons or evenings, once you meet the seller, is having to pass through the agency: "What a shame: why, we both could have saved. I on the percentage for the agent, you on the agent's markup." The point of this is to set the stage for a friendly exchange.

In the final stages, in our case, the discussion was carried on about the exchange of currency with the owner of the agency listening behind what had seemed a closed door. . . . Americans, as is well known, have a great deal of money, as do the British, and college professors are wonderfully paid. Everyone seemed to know this but us, both of whom were indeed professors. At all events, when you finally arrive at the notary, you have a friendly discussion, and then suddenly the phone is said to ring. Now we never heard anything at all, but the phone was thought to be ringing, at least by the notary and the seller. The notary exits and this is the point at which you delicately slip to the seller an envelope containing many bills (one-third to one-half) that is called "the amount under the table." This is so you will not have to declare it or pay on it. The notary comes back in, wreathed in smiles; his phone call must have gone well. And he gets a percentage of the sale. You sign all the endless papers, hand over the check for what you are declaring (or, preferably, the actual cash), and then the seller takes you out to lunch. Or has you at home, with everyone there too wreathed in smiles.

Of course, at this point, we had already started wondering about those tiles not on the roof, those parts of the would-be floor not in the floor, and that land around the cabanon that is actually not ours because the seller still owns the cherry trees until they die, including the terrain upon which they sit. On which we will sit only, as it were, being upon borrowed land. There is also no electricity and no water except from the picturesque spring, indeed, and little did we know how that works. We were rapidly to find out; but in any case, the cabanon is bought, the lunch is very good, and I like very much—coming from another South as I do—to see people smiling.

This is an extraordinary place to have acquired a spot in which to live. It has a long intellectual tradition. From miles around, the Mont Ventoux—the Windy Mountain—is used as a landmark. It was Petrarch's mountain, which brought back Roman times to him and made him value differently the idea of place. La Fontaine de Vaucluse, near L'Isle-sur-Sorgue, not far away, was the spring he cared about, associating it with his love of Laura. The "closed valley" of the Vaucluse (*Vallis clausus*) stretches between those landmarks, between a spring and a mountain. Thomas Jefferson too loved the Ventoux in his time, and remembered Petrarch's love of it as the basis for his own. It is, and has always been thought of, as a special mountain. Bare of vegetation on top, and extensive in its stretch around, it rivets the eyes and the imagination.

That the Mont Ventoux is a choice breeding ground for vipers in no way harms its evocative reputation. They are used to make the antivenom against viper bites: the circular logic stirs the imagination, as do many of the aspects of the Ventoux. Bare as it is, it is held responsible for many events in the region: for the mistral wind and for the clear sky, for too many visitors and for the regional wine, flinty and fruity at once, for visitations of various spirits and for poetic myths. The Ventoux is marked up its impressively winding road by the gravestones of those intrepid bikers who made it only part way up. When we first came, our neighbor Jean-Marie said to me with reverence the name: "Simpson. . . . " And the same evening, he brought me a little book I still treasure, with the poems of Frederic Mistral, leader of the Felibrige group in Avignon. Those details are linked forever in my mind: this language, this mountain, and a kind of courage.

In our early days here, I thought I would find myself ambling over in my Deux Chevaux to the other side of the mountain to Malaucène to learn Provençal and to speak the patois of the region; I shall not be doing that, and the trips I make in the language and in my car have a more modest radius still. As it turns out, I didn't need to make that trip to Malaucène.

From the beginning, in this other South, the southern France that is Provence, it was always the olive trees that mattered most to us. Glittering in the Provençal sun, they stand tall. Not as tall as the oaks, of course, nor

as the cherry trees lined up stretching out from my small field house near
the Mont Ventoux, the Cabanon Biska, so named because the original owner
so many years ago had been known for his complaining: *bisquer* in the patois
of the country.

Complaining is thought of as a good preventative measure in this region,
one of the poorer parts of France. You complain about the wind, the rain,
the sun, the drought, the rifts made in the cherries by the rain, the high price
of living, and the low price of selling your cherries and your work. . . . Not
to complain would be to tempt fate, and it seems to take little tempting. You
would be likely to attract evil fortune for having nothing to lament or for
not lamenting it. There are indeed a great many things to regret, and more
are being invented every day. Some are traditional, forming the mainstays
of conversation at the grocery store: the great north wind, or the mistral,
purifiant and clarifying, is powerful enough to cause marriages to split apart,
to give you a headache, and to sour the milk. But it clears everything off,
and up. "After the mistral," we say of a superb day, "of course, it is after the
mistral." The south wind, or sirocco, the unhealthy wind, is likely to put
everyone in a bad mood. Too much or too little sun, too much or too little
rain ruins the grapes, the melons, the tomatoes. And it is customary to complain of the intrusions into the region by foreigners—Belgians, Germans,
Swiss, Dutch, English, Americans, or Parisians, the most foreign of all, from
the point of view of my French neighbors. *Tout ça, c'est des estrangers, quoi.*
As for us, perhaps because of René Char, perhaps because we had so much
to do on our cabanon, we had the great joy of never feeling like strangers in
this land.

Hidden in its almond and cherry trees, marked off by rosemary shrubs and
by dry stone walls that stand above the Roman walls at their base, our
cabanon is situated far up a hill, leading up to another hill, a favorite spot
for climbing, on horse and foot; a Roman road marks the way down, its
stones worn and with faint inscriptions covered over. You can take it, down
through the underbrush, when you have time. . . . But then our cabanon
itself requires its own climbing. To arrive at the upper part, you must go
around the house, up the hill it is situated on, or now, up the steep stone
steps my cousins have built directly outside the kitchen. When these were
just a gleam in their eye, never in mine, I lamented over the fate of my sunny

corner, full of ivy. To be sure, convenience wins out, even over a sunny corner made by the ivy-covered yellow stone wall, the two intimately connected, like the mountain and the wind.

Of that yellow earth and gray white stone, the cabanon is built with one room atop another, just barely holding itself together with the crumbling mortar here and there, and topped by old red tiles on the roof—now replenished and anchored by gray rocks. The tiles tend to shift in the mistral, and from time to time, some rain pours through, until someone climbs on the roof to take a look. Intertwined with the stone and mortar, the quick-growing ivy would eventually knock the tiles off the roof, if a neighbor did not make his way up a tall ladder to clip the top. This is called: "giving the cabanon a haircut," or shearing it a bit, just as you would a sheep:

Il faut tondre le cabanon,

someone would say. "Whose turn is it?" there is always something to be done here, by whoever is here. For example, the land around the cabanon would fill with brambles every year, and every year I would clear them out, cutting them back with a small curved tree saw I loved, its wooden handle smoothed by its years of service. When I had enough brambles to make a load, I would take the long three-pronged fork of olive wood, the *fourche* I had gotten in the hill town of Buis-les-Baronnies, gather them up, and carry them away over my head. It felt like a moral duty, like "liberating" the olive trees from the vines that are eager to mount them and choke off the air. I rose at five in the morning to remove all the growth around and in these trees, because René Char, the poet I had loved and trusted, had come here to the cabanon and told me how the olive was jealous of anything in its way. It needed its space to grow in and be content. I had believed him, I still do.

There were other things I would do because of what he said. I would gather the branches from the sweet-smelling shrubs around our little stone house and make a bath for us all, to ward off insects, he had said. He knew—and we knew he was always right—that it would ward off much more. Protecting us from things we didn't even suspect possible, that might have harmed us. He gave us a talisman of stone to put on our chimney mantel, and cards with his sayings on them to stick on our plaster walls. He kept a picture of our children in his bookcase, and we kept the stones and sayings he bestowed on us.

When the spring that gave us our water dried up, he told us what to say to it: "Spring, our friend, run gently for us." Hilary and Matthew went up to speak to the spring, exactly as he had said. He must have meant us to speak in the Provençal language, as he could, or it would have worked. Yet we didn't lose our trust, in him, or in this part of Provence we lived in because of him, and loved, mostly for the same reason, at least at first.

We were fortunate that no evil befell us. For we were all alone here, surrounded, in a land strange to us, by strangers. That they later became our friends was a wonderful happening whose source we never questioned. Our poet had told us that we were to be forever *Pays,* part of his country, along with him, and so we were bound to be at home here, as much as the olive trees. As much as the ivy that grows thick up the walls, as the light that falls differently in the different months on the large field up to the spring that you walk to surrounded by the sounds of the birds and crickets.

That great and windy mountain of the Ventoux, from which the mistral blows, inhabited by a long and precious tradition, has not always been treated as it deserves. When it was about to be besmirched by nuclear installations, Picasso, in a fireman's helmet, and Char, in an Indian headdress, protested violently, to no avail. The installation sits upon it "like a suppository," as Char put it, irreverently and exactly.

Char taught us all, in those years: how to build and how to preserve— walls and roofs, but also the simplest of things. How you keep butter cool in a porous pot hung high in the breeze; and how you keep poetry living, leaning it against a dry house: *une maison sèche.* Its stones hold together without mortar, like the *bories* of Ligurian times—so everything in the poem has to fit, exactly. He told us endless stories about Provençal heroes and monsters and friends. Stories about the Resistance, of course, in which he was known as "Le capitaine Alexandre," and about his life and poetry.

Downstairs in the kitchen, we laid red tiles, over which some ivy leaves blow in through the door from time to time, a door that is never closed. A yellow cloth is usually spread over the farm table, sizable enough to seat a good-sized bunch of family or friends in the tiny room in bad weather. A bunch of dried flowers, blue and yellowish, with a few sprigs of white, rests in the round iron cartwheel suspended from a wooden peg at the side, and overhead hangs another larger cartwheel to hold the net bags of vegetables: purple aubergine, green squash, yellow onions. On the table, some old, uneven wooden platters and heavy bowls: piles of bright tomatoes, green beans, peaches and apricots. Different sizes of potatoes are heaped up in the woven baskets against the wall, where we keep our assortment of onions and long tresses of garlic, with a few lemons. Leaning nearby is the wooden pitching fork from Buis-les-Baronnies, about which Char wrote a dancing poem, "Dansons aux Baronnies," so it means more to all of us.

Old iron pieces found in the field have been set in the plaster to suspend the heavier cooking implements, the pots and pans, near the smallish gas stove, whose burners are lit with one of those long lighters with a spark at the end. A smattering of wooden spoons stands in an earthenware pot beneath them. To feed the stove and the little hot water tank, it takes immense gas bottles purchased in the village, and too heavy for me to lift. When they are empty, they can be rolled down to the road with great effort. Against the far wall, a tall open cabinet of cherrywood reaches to the ceiling, with bottles, glasses, and heavy Provençal tablecloths below and, above, three shelves with rails, where yellow plates stand on their edges behind the piles of matte brown or dull greenish blue plates and bowls. Sometimes a potter who stays in or visits the cabanon leaves a piece, as writers leave one of their books in the upstairs bookcase, full to overflowing.

These pieces in our kitchen have a somber sheen to them, glazed in places, and matte in others—they feel at once rough and smooth to the touch, and what is served in them seems to taste different from what is placed on the light brown earthenware *grès* plates I bought upon first arriving. In the cabinet our neighbors call our *meuble,* our piece of furniture, for indeed we have only that one, there are some other pieces: a teapot from Aix, of an old yellow, with tiny red roses, and two teacups for favorite friends who might drop in some late afternoon. It is then that the squat black teapot made in Vaison-la-Romaine comes out: it is badly conceived, spilling water out its spout on the unwary hand, but I use it warily.

Upstairs, in the tiny room where the owner used to nap while the horse dozed below, you see just a bed, a little wooden table, a wooden armoire in the corner, and a trunk covered with the same Provençal material as the bed, at once luminous and dark, deep gold and black in a pattern of paisley and stripe. As for the great beams holding up the roof, an extra one has been placed on either side of the one in the center, because the latter is almost entirely scooped out by carpenter ants, in spite of my constant (if irregular) attention to it with Xylophène, the anti-ant product you squirt into all the little holes that prove the presence or erstwhile presence of said ants. A presence first detected by the little piles of wood droppings on the floor or the books below.

Upon the white plaster walls that have to be patched on occasion, there are taped bouquets of dried flowers and posters of ancient stone heads from Cluny, of Maurice Denis and the Nabis, and various museum exhibitions. Behind the bed, in a large Pisanello I brought back from Verona, a horse turns away its head, and young faces look out with what I imagine to be affection. On the side wall hangs a series of straw hats, for me and for visitors to protect against the unpardoning sun:

On the hearth in the corner, as on all the bookshelves, stands a great jug of dried lavender, much of it having come from Char's garden, where he would pick great bundles of it at the end of a day spent together—perhaps one of those days when he had grilled lamb chops for us in the chimney by his desk and served them with the lightly sautéed eggplant over which he had put a *coulis de tomate*. Afterward, he would grind the coffee, holding the square wooden grinder between his knees and turning the metal handle on top, until the little drawer at the bottom was filled.

It might have been one of those days when he had gone behind his house to pick melons and potatoes with our children and given them their *goûter* of chocolate and biscuits, perhaps one of those days when he had to put a bandage on Hilary's leg, scraped in the briars when she had taken his beloved dog, Tigron, to walk in the fields: a good day. When he came to visit our cabanon, it was because Matthew, a particular friend of his, had fallen off the wall of the upper part onto the lower and just barely survived. René Char, mountainous in body as in spirit, chose to sit on an upturned grape crate, so as not to split the canvas of our only chairs. He looked about, and his eyes filled with tears:

Cela me rappelle le maquis, he said. It reminds me of the maquis.

Logs burn in the fireplace in the winter, and we might toast marshmallows on some of the old iron cooking tools hanging on both sides, along with the pokers and long forks. As for the rust-colored stains above the mantel, we were told that if you rub them with twenty-seven cloves of garlic, the stains will disappear. Having lived here more than thirty summers and falls, I have not tried this remedy, attached now to all these traces of the past. In the wall, a small square wooden door, painted yellow, marks a cabinet with shelves deep in the thick stone wall. A few leaves gather on the floor when the mistral sweeps through the little openings for windows, but no one minds. In the niche of the *fenestron,* a small horizontal slot once used as a lookout upon the path, and now closed in, we stack a pile of books for reading in bed.

Outside, against the wall, is an irregular stone basin from which, so they say, the horse used to drink, over which hangs a grapevine. The grapes ripen at the end of the summer, more purple by the day. A large table is placed in the field here, among the grasses and the wild flowers, where you can sit looking at cherry trees at the end of the field, and the changing light, from early morning to late darkness under the stars. The ground of the field is uneven, and lovely in its unevenness: daisies grow, and early in the summer, poppies, and some bluish grass; a few sparse vines, growing back after they were pulled up when I bought the field, poke up through the assorted flowers.

In the near distance, up the slope, live our friends Malcolm and Janet, the winegrowers, whose red roof can just be glimpsed at a distance. The top of the hill beyond them can be seen from the table, from the windows in the upper room: it is the central point of the landscape, and of its history. With a more modest history, our cabanon has made its peace.

All the things we use for our daily living contain their past: the *tian,* the large pottery vessel that was used traditionally to hold everything from vegetables for the ratatouille to the *fruits confits* from Apt, now holding our provision of fresh herbs for today's cooking; the boot scraper set into the lower wall, by the door, where we place our melons in the sun; the old wheel of the cart set into our ceiling, from which most of our vegetables and some dried flowers are hanging; the spokes those wheels used to contain within them now jutting out from our walls, holding the cooking tongs and forks; the hollow stone the horse drank from, now the wash basin; the little opening in the wall that was a one-way window, now a bookcase; the old tree trunks now the poles set up to hold the *canisse* overhead to protect the table from the sun—these are ways of living history.

The first six summers, we seemed, all of us, to be always building. Removing the twenty-four wheelbarrows of manure from our little kitchen, which the horse had originally occupied in the daytime before going home, we put the great slabs of red stone there. We repaired the upstairs floor with its holes, where the boards were giving way at last. We fixed the walls, all of us cementing and plastering with much of the neighborhood standing about, feet in a circle around us as we bent over our task. The silence was usually unbroken until one part was finished.

C'est pas comme ça qu'il fallait faire!

It's not like *that* we were supposed to do it, and no one told us? Now they do, all at once, with large grins. The process is repeated, same silence, same grins, same teasing, and we become friends. Forever, I expect. This must have been the testing time, when it just seemed like cementing and plastering: in any case, those two skills stay with you, like the neighbors. For from next door there began to appear, more and more frequently, the whole family, bearing gifts. All the Conils, the *cultivateurs* next door, would take the path from their larger house down to our far smaller cabanon to make us welcome. Some green beans in a little pot, a jar of freshly put up apricot jam, and later in the summer, a bunch of the first grapes, dewy and purple. We were really working now, becoming part of the hill.

At night the gas lamps for camping would splutter over our soup and our reading, and we would sink to sleep happy, and exhausted by our labor. And sometimes, in the dark of night, or first thing in the morning before work, a neighbor would come to bring us something else, just to chat, or to give us a hand. We felt ourselves privileged, loved, accepted.

We are here all summer; these summers seem not to stretch out any more endlessly, as I thought they used to; they have pieces to them, and most of these pieces are as brightly colored as the old-patterned sturdy cotton Provençal cloths I put over the table downstairs under the trees, and upstairs, over the line in the open field before the cherry trees. They are variously yellow, red, and blue, and the material takes no ironing. I used just to wash them out in *Génie,* that sweet-smelling soap powder you can use in cold water, for hand washing. *Sans frotter,* it says, takes no rubbing. Indeed it doesn't. I love hanging those bright cloths, with their clean smell now, on the lines stretching over the wild mint, crushed under my feet and fragrant, until the cloths feel crisp from the sun and sometimes the mistral.

"High summer," what a beautiful expression. All summer long, our neighbors, some French, some not, will be coming to the cabanon for a pastis, bringing friends and problems, stories and gossip, their teasing and affectionate warmth. You listen to everything over two or three glasses of this opaque liquid, its licorice cool with the chilled water, in the hour of drinks that may stretch from seven to ten, after the heat dies down, under the waning light.

As we sit there, feeling life going by, as the trees sway in the mistral wind, and the sunlight falls unevenly on the leaves of the cherry trees and on the irregular grasses, blue and green, the talk continues around us, as if always picking up from last summer. Light flickers on the faces around the table, against the ivy-covered wall. Now the neighbors are telling their daily and no less wonderful tales about things near and far, waving their hands about and delighting in the telling.

When we first came, our next-door neighbors, the Conils, were the ones who welcomed us daily; Jean-Marie, tiny in stature, with his keen eyes slightly crossed, was the one who brought the first grapes in a little bunch and the first beans in a dull green heap; he took the children, Matthew and Hilary, to see baby wild boars, always calling to them:

Eh! Mathieu! Hilary! O là!

to let us know he was coming, when he arrived for a pastis at eleven or a coffee at four. He brought me some Mistral when I read no Provençal—but the point was made; I loved poetry, and the gesture mattered more than the language. Here it often does. Of this neighbor who first welcomed me by cutting a branch that tapped against my roof, by loving my children, what can I say? As the villagers say of him, *"Jean-Marie, c'est un pur."* Like our poet, our neighbor is true to himself and vivid in his warmth. Small as he is, he dominates any room he is in, and this hill is marked as surely by his presence, and that of his father and forefathers behind him, as is the Vaucluse by its poets and its rivers, the Ventoux by its mountain.

Diable! he will say, when we attempt to tell him something, *Diable!* It serves for good and bad, ordinary and extraordinary, and I have never heard anyone else pronounce it quite like he did, or upon so many occasions. We used to spend hours listening to his anecdotes, all of us. Now, retired from his tractor, he has changed his style of living. We sometimes go to have dinner with him and his wife, Augusta, whom I am now—after these twenty years—to call "Tata," as the children do ("remember if you need anything, neighbors are there for that!"). His actual dinner now takes place from 7 to 7:05, after which he retires to watch some violent thing on television, all the same keeping an eye on the women in the kitchen. That is to say, in this case, his wife and me, gossiping over a tisane: she likes *tilleul,* or lime-tree fragrance; I like *verveine,* or verbena.

Tata is a superb cook and shares her kitchen as her recipes. Her life has not been easy; they had no water but from a cistern until two years ago, and she raised four children, working with them, and feeding everyone. At the time of the vendange, she would have to feed all the workers, and yet do the grape harvesting herself also; her life, as she tells me with a smile, has always been taking care of people. First, Jean-Marie's father, then the children: Serge, Alain, Ghislaine, and Claude. For years, supper at night, as in many of the farmers' homes, was bread soup (*la panade*). When times were slightly better, there might be bouillon over the bread . . .

Ah, Marianne. Je suis si fatiguée.

Down the stone stairs too high to be reassuring, the table for work and meals and tea, and for sitting around with a pastis or a syrup, is the center of our evenings if we're not too many (in which case we dine upstairs in the field). It rests upon flat white yellow stones, in a sort of *tonnelle,* or shelter, amid the trees interweaving their leaves, beyond which I have just laid a square of old stones, fitting the straight sides together into the ground. The table is covered with a bright Provençal cloth, blue in the morning, and red or yellow in the evening, depending on my mood; it is surrounded by chairs with woven straw seats, upon which I place large straw hats that usually hang on my wall upstairs, if I think those coming to lunch will need protection from the sun that beams even through the slats of the bamboo cover, or *canisse,* overhead. The slats, held together by thin wires, rest on a structure of logs and slender tree trunks: a honeysuckle vine is making its way up, and I try to overlook the fact that its sweet odor will attract my deadly enemy later on in the summer, the mighty wasp, to which I am more than mightily allergic. To the nearby hospital I have been taken in the middle of several repasts, but I try to forget that, and cherish the honeysuckle for the moment. Later, we will see.

Sun shines on the ivy, on the side of the house, and on the Roman wall by the table. Telling me, over a pastis, how once he was tempted to dig down to his Roman wall, Jean-Marie, a cigarette in the corner of his mouth, says:

> Ah yes, I'd have liked to see my wall. But then I realized the cherry tree needed water—you have to choose the living over the dead.

So he covered the Roman times back up.

Along the road, beyond another hedge of rosemary bushes upon a stone wall ("of dry stone in a dry land"), at all hours of the day and night come a few cars, a motorbike or two, and occasional walkers, ready for the climb uphill. But generally it is peaceful among the trees. My olive trees are growing again, after a bad frost a few years ago, and there are the cherry trees, of which I have given the fruit to my neighbors Serge and Alain; they sell them at the markets, rushing them there from one evening to the next day. There are a few almond trees, with their green bittersweet nuts, a few tall bushes with small black berries, several rosemary shrubs along the walls, a few clumps of thyme alongside them, and then some sage; there is an occasional oak, and a spring that has provided a good deal of Pagnol-type drama over the years.

When they were little, our children used to go up with great jugs to get the water there for drinking, washing, living; this was formerly the water for the sheep, and each neighbor had a partial right to it. Like "passage rights," water rights are oddly complicated. All of this has to do with arriving at the correct time to draw one's water, with or without one's animals. At our spring, the Biska spring, the water used to be rationed out to the neighbors: one could water his sheep on Thursdays and Mondays, two to four, another on Tuesdays and Fridays, four to six, and so on. At one point it was three and a half days for the goats, three and a half for the vines: at this point, about 1944 or 1945, says Tata, a terrible thing happened one day, beyond the ordinary quarrels about when it is your turn and when mine.

> Tata, you must go home immediately, said the father of the man who sold us the cabanon. Go home right now. Hurry.

Whatever for? I just got here to take care of my goats.

They have been grazing on my vines, and have killed them all. Go home before I lose my temper: I am leaving now to go home myself.

And he did. So did she, heartsick over the incident—those vines were now lost forever. As she tells me the story now, it is bitter but funny, like many of her stories about our neighbors in common, or about my spring, whose water was always thought of as curative. Jean-Marie's father would come up every day, convinced it would cure his sniffles if he simply anointed his nose with it.

Its magic properties were less visible to me than its fickle behavior. When the ground shifted and the spring would not come to the surface, or when the spring would dry up, the problems were dramatic—I would go down on my mobylette to get water from La Brèche and bring it back up in jugs in my market basket on the back of the bike. When the water was seen to have really stopped running, and all the dowsers in the region were busy finding new sources of water, René Char came again to have a word with our spring.

Friend spring, he said, run for me. *Source amie, coule pour moi.*

It must have listened a bit, to him and to the children, who went after him and repeated his prayer—for years after, we would ram out the spring with a long rod (Sears Roebuck), and have the water come to us in long plastic tubes. It was hot, and we preferred the fresh spring taste, so we would continue to go up with our bottles for our drinking supply. But then came the water from the town: vastly less picturesque, and vastly simpler.

POSTCARDS

But this early life of ours, in Provence as in New York, rushed by. And now, for me, only a few scenes from our early years stand out, against a background blurred by time. They feel now like a series of postcards from long ago.

In San Jose, Costa Rica, with a smell of coffee everywhere, there is a downpour from 3:30 to 4:00 every afternoon. The mountains around the vol-

cano Irazu are high in the mist. One day we take the train down to the coast, to Puerto Limon. In a little hotel there, the waiter asks Peter how we want our eggs:

Como quieren sus huevos?

and we would never know whether he meant how did we want our eggs for breakfast or whether it was an ironic expression meaning something like have you had enough? It was an odd recall of our honeymoon and that doomed egg.

In Lawrence, Kansas, where we are teaching as visiting professors, we are going to a triple feature at the drive-in, something like The Flies, Some Sharks, *and* The Monster Within. *We have a great pail of homemade popcorn in the front seat and in the backseat our beloved dog, Melissa, half coyote and half German shepherd. We have gotten the dog to make our live-in friend from Peter's boyhood happy: instead, Ron sliced off his finger in the delicatessen, burned the sheets with a candle, and finally has returned to England. Peter and I continue with Melissa.*

In Oaxaca on a springtime trip, standing on a high plateau, Peter is reading some Stevenson aloud, to me, but mostly I think to himself. He is always attracted to the idea of wandering, I know that. Once, in Paris, he spoke of just setting out alone, on foot. But we always found each other after either of us would set out.

On some Greek island, he is smiling broadly, and I take his picture. Like sunlight, his face to me, under his shock of hair. I love him.

In a little hotel in Brittany, he is reading to the children, after we have all had some of an araignée de mer, *a large crab with many very long legs. They are grinning at* The Narnia Chronicles *Peter is reading to them.*

We are in Rome, and he is speaking Italian to Hilary and Matthew, slowly, and making large meaningful gestures. They are laughing. Me too.

We are in Paris, we are taking the children to the Luxembourg to play in the Jardin d'enfants. But we have forgotten their goûter for midafternoon, that sacred snack of chocolate and bread; I know it is my fault. Hilary's frog has escaped from the log of wood we have in our apartment. We are having a picnic by the Seine and looking for it there, improbably. Peter and I are arguing, somewhere on the Left Bank between the streets Gay-Lussac and Saint-Jacques. We separate, furious, and turn back, laughing, and embrace.

We are holding the children on our shoulders during the peace parades in Washington, during the Vietnam war; we are worrying about their night-mares after the fires in their school during the disturbances following Kent State; and we are eternally, in New York, going with them to the boathouse in Central Park, them on the back of our bikes, them on their own little bikes. We feel ourselves a family.

Our boathouse. We lock our bikes to the rail or to each other's, side by side, the little red plaid seat and the little green plaid seat on the back of our black bikes, Matthew behind me and Hilary behind Peter.

In the big freeze, we are walking, all four of us holding hands, across the lake by the boathouse, surrounded by snowshoes and short skis. This is the clearest of the memories.

Before we had children, we used to have our coffee and rolls at the Wollman Rink, where we pretended to ice-skate, before, during, and sometimes after making the icy rounds, falling a few times, and clutching the rail more desperately by far than the skaters around us.

What about a coffee?

one of us would ask, and we were happy. We gave up the rink far before it gave up, but the boathouse was to be forever. More than us, we knew. Peter would read Petrarch sonnets to me; I'd read him Wallace Stevens.

And then:

What about a boat?

Whichever of us said it, we would laugh, pick up our book bags, and rush out, trusting in that sudden excitement of the setting out, smiling at each other, always afresh on the lake. The boathouse and the lake were home for all of us.

It all went by so quickly, leaving memories and nothing more.

Harmon Chadbourn Rorison (Father) in his plane, with the Kosciusko Squadron, before World War I

Margaret Devereux Lippitt Rorison (Mother) at Wrightsville Beach, North Carolina

Margaret Lippitt Rorison (Peg) fly-fishing on the Gaspé
Peninsula

Peter and I at commencement exercises for City University of New York

Father, Mother, and Hilary Brooke Caws, outside our beach cottage on the sound at Wrightsville Beach

Peter, Hilary, and myself outside my family's home on Oleander

Hilary and Matthew outside the cabanon in the Vaucluse

René Char, showing Matthew and Hilary how a stalk of lavender is formed, in his garden at Les Busclats, L'Ile-sur-Sorgue

Hilary and Matthew in a Brittany forest

Hilary on the beach at Cabourg, Marcel Proust's "Balbec"

Matthew and Peter on a mountain lake

Hilary reading, at Virginia Woolf's Monk's House, when Sarah Bird
Wright was living there (photograph courtesy of Sarah Bird Wright)

Sarah Bird Wright in a wheat field in the Vaucluse

On the porch of our cottage at Wrightsville Beach

In my Paris hotel window, overlooking the Théâtre de l'Odéon

Peter and myself on our bikes, near the boathouse in Central Park

Matthew in our last 2CV, on the road outside our cabanon, in the Vaucluse

Hilary and I in our Breton sweaters, by a Brittany beach

Patrick Cullen after a Bach concert at Lincoln
Center

Gerhard Joseph, my colleague, in the Vaucluse

Patricia Terry with Kala, in San Diego

Christopher Prendergast, at Wrightsville Beach

With the French-Egyptian poet Edmond Jabès at
Cerisy-la-Salle, Normandy

Carolyn Heilbrun and myself, at the Modern Language Association annual meeting

With my neighbor Augusta (Tata) Conil, at the cabanon in the Vaucluse (photograph courtesy of Matthew Caws)

Boyce Bennett, on our trip to Turkey

Matthew in Nada Surf mode (photograph courtesy of Pascale Duranel)

Hilary raising a glass of wine, outside the cabanon

Four

Separating

I HAVE TO REMEMBER HOW it was, how it really was. How, if it had gone on, it would always have been. In the small college town we were first in, East Lansing, Michigan, and then in Lawrence, Kansas, in fact everywhere we went, student after student clustered around Peter. Of course, and it did not improve things that I understood why. I was shy, and he spoke. I felt drab, and he was colorful; clumsy, and he was at ease. I was seldom at ease, except speaking or teaching or writing. Odd, how the professional side of things is least hard. Something about passion that gets you through.

Like everyone, we had relational problems, to ourselves and others. Not all his, by any means. Early on in our relationship, in Le Petit Cluny, our favorite Paris café, I noticed a particular shade of green socks above some thin-soled brown shoes beneath sharply creased beige flannel trousers. The trousers were adorning the spare frame of a well-tanned Yves Montand type. I, however, only had eyes for his shoes. French shoes, I said to myself, I shall get some for Peter. I made the mistake of saying aloud, just loud enough for him to hear:

Peter, look at those!

Peter was, quite against his habit, taken by a moment of jealousy, or his equivalent thereof. He saw me staring at the shoes, assumed something or, perhaps, wanted to assume something, and turned my chair so that I remained facing the gentleman with the shoes. He must have known I would turn scarlet with embarrassment. I did. Mortified, I could not move, and could not seem to explain to Peter his mistake; maybe I thought it was mine also.

This was only one of such entanglements, closely followed by what I now think of as the Sanskrit sequence, an attachment I formed, wrongly—easy to say, no matter how true. A linguistics professor whom Peter had consulted about some early historical documents. It complicated itself, until the three of us, Peter and Professor Gupta and I all went off to London together, then to Paris. Then Peter made his statement:

Mary Ann, I am leaving you.

Peter went off on the boat train from the Gare du Nord for his native London, refusing to let me join him, turning me over, or so it seemed to me, to the other man. The lovely girl seated by him on the train was just striking up a conversation when the train pulled out: more of those pangs in the heart that sickened me.

Then Professor Gupta fled for India. I felt I had been set up for a betrayal by both men and by my own chaos, unsure, and alone. After a week, I went off after Peter, whom I never managed to stop loving and knowing I loved. Did he ever pardon me? I never knew, but somehow hoped our having children together after that might work the miracle. It didn't, and nothing would have.

When it was Peter's turn, it happened precisely as it does in novels, when the young mother is recovering after her first birth. Peter, as I said, has a precise mind. I found out only later. Then the pain of knowing he was spending the weekend with his secretary was doubled by finding out it had gone on so long.

> It is a fall Sunday. Hilary, a year old, is playing in her Babygro outfit on the rug. The autumn sun is streaming in on its pink and the reds and blues of the faded Persian pattern. I can't stop crying.
>
> I try to find the secretary's number, sure she will understand. I cannot find it. Will she be living with my husband? Pain is imprinted on the Babygro, but I must above all not let it get to my daughter.
>
> I can't concentrate on writing, reading, thinking, preparing classes. I think I am going mad, and that I don't have time to.

GETTING HELP

When I thought I could bear it no longer, I got the name of a psychiatrist from my gynecologist, who looked at me oddly.

Are you in a tough spot?

he asked sympathetically, looking at me over the top of his half-rimmed glasses.

Very,

I just managed to say. And went immediately to see the psychoanalyst he had suggested. Not without noticing that my doctor was stapling to my folder a statement that I could read even upside down, Marital Difficulties. Suicidal. Indeed.

Never having been to consult anyone like that, I felt terribly embarrassed even about getting to his waiting room, on the fourth floor of a Park Avenue building. The elevator man looked at me hard when I said: "Dr. Wilkie, please." In the waiting room, someone was sedulously reading *Psychology Today*, avoiding any eye contact. Good idea. When it was her turn to go in, she took her coat with her, for it was a one-way passage.

Forty minutes later I heard her leave through the other door, then heard a rustling, as of a paper being read. Dr. Wilkie was catching up on the *New York Times* in between patients, and having a smoke. After ten minutes exactly, he came in to get me, cigarette still in the corner of his mouth. A nice face, if somewhat stern, and a three-piece suit. A three-piece suit, and here it was March, with the spring almost beginning. I was not surprised to see his Phi Beta Kappa key delicately protruding from some pocket. This was not an auspicious start.

He settled me in a large comfortable red leather chair, just like his, put his feet in their black loafers up on an ottoman, red leather to match the chairs, and smiled comfortingly, waiting to hear my problem. I was, I said, having a "sort of hard time."

All of a sudden, I hear myself talking: I am precisely imprecise. No wonder Peter was irritated: always the same clothes, always the same friends, always the same conversation, he would say. Won't you ever change?

We are in the kitchen, sitting at the bar, and I am recounting the day's events, trying not to make too much of something, or act as if I know too much. Peter is laughing. He says: look how you water down your expressions, listen to you: "sort of," "kind of," "I guess," "I think." Why don't you know your own mind?

Dr. Wilkie smiled again encouragingly, and fingered his key. I was suddenly aware that I was using just the words Peter teased me for using. And he was right: "sort of" gives no one any confidence, yourself or the person you are speaking to. Peter really had tried to be helpful, hadn't he?

Maybe I shouldn't be here; I don't want to complain about my husband. But I have to continue my story, if only just to say why I am here. I wish I weren't, I wish I didn't have to be. What would happen if I got up and left?

Dr. Wilkie chain-smoked, worried about the air conditioner, whose noise he "could not stand." But he looked like someone to trust, in spite of his foibles—he, after all, was not trying to do himself in by walking in front of traffic, seeing how sharp the tips of the iron spikes were atop the railings, taking pills. . . . His remarks were helpful, witty, and above all, intelligent. This was not so bad. I felt I was making sense, he was making sense, and maybe the situation would have its own sense if I could just see it.

Until I remarked on a fact that seemed of minor importance to me compared to the rest. I am in fact a mild narcoleptic. I fall asleep when I concentrate the hardest, at lectures I like, in front of the paintings I most love, and, more dangerously, sometimes at the wheel of a car or anywhere in it: vibrations of the motor, or something like that, very soothing. That is often the way I get my rest, since I have always had to work in the middle of almost every night.

Through the recital of my woes, of the chill of Peter, of our double faithlessness, of my alcoholic hero father, all of them, Dr. Wilkie maintained a relaxed position. He was taking notes from time to time, but without any particular facial or verbal expression. Until suddenly, at the mention of my falling asleep in cars and lectures, he sat bolt upright with a start.

Narcolepsy! You are a narcoleptic!

I listened to his exclamation, astounded at the change in his demeanor. When I had a brain scan, it showed up as definite narcolepsy, but minor. I was not a raving danger, just a little one. And so I did not drive. No problem in New York.

Yes,

I said, wanting to reassure him. Even a psychiatrist needs reassurance, right?

Mild case, though. So I am told.
Let me tell you what we know about its control by the mind,

began Dr. Wilkie, rapidly warming up to his subject now.

Here is what you must do.

With that, he diagnosed this disease as coming from the depths of my troubled personality and instantly curable by the following method. What I must do, he said, was very simple. Just get a very large car.

Then, with great confidence, you must take it out on the road and practice not being afraid. All this week, you will drive every day on some side roads, in the Village if you like, or somewhere quiet, early in the morning. Then next week, you start on the East River Drive. See? Then you are cured.

I saw, but remained unconvinced. The last time I drove a large car on a highway, I almost killed us all. The car swerved out of control as I nodded and sailed across the highway, until Matthew awoke me by taking the steering wheel from behind. I don't know what Peter was doing, but I felt guilty and have ever since. I was not eager to repeat the experience, even with my unhappiness at living.

Yes, sir.
Don't be formal with me. Would you like to call me Lionel?

asked Dr. Wilkie.

Personally, I never could imagine liking to call anyone Lionel, but nodded my head slightly. Sure, I could do that. But not the big car. He hadn't understood. I rose to my feet after forty minutes, and shook his hand.

Shall we make it every Wednesday and Friday, then? Ten to ten forty?

This was the crunch. It was like cocktail parties. It was like the South. I was supposed to be wanting to go on. I did not long to repeat this experience, in spite of his kindness.

I, um . . .

I began. He waited.

I was just trying out something,

I said feebly.

Would you excuse me please?

And wrote my check and left. Maybe some time in the future I would return to see Dr. Wilkie, but not now.

We tried to weather that one. When my fits of jealousy would overcome me, Peter, always rational, handled it and me as best he could. He wasn't exactly warm, but then he wasn't exactly cold either: he was just neutral. That should have been right, but it wasn't enough for me:

Mary Ann,

he would say calmly,

Mary Ann, I do think you are overreacting.

I do think I was not overreacting, just reacting, as anyone would. Perhaps more hot temperedly, yet I always felt provoked to it. I remember such a scene in Central Park, when I unleashed all my feelings at him:

Mary Ann, not in front of the children, please!

Peter even raised his voice slightly, showing just how horrified he was. Shocked by my misbehavior.

He was right: I was plainly hysterical, yet I managed to continue living somehow. Over and over, I "mortified" myself and my family. Particularly Peter. "Mortified"—his word. How else could he have put it, of course, but the resonance of "mort" and death kept haunting me. I was putting an end to our family. I had begun the drama, and was continuing it, while Peter, always calm, was justified. Mortified and justified. I can find no other words. Having spent so much time in my life on words, these words, inadequate, spun about in my head, and were all I had to focus on.

> *Jealousy has no words adequate to it. Being beside yourself with rage: that is the closest I can come. You are beside yourself. Fear, inadequacy, torment, hell, what? I cannot get to it. The gestures and threats, suicidal and homicidal, might have been all a show to myself or to him: if I had meant it, would I not have succeeded?*

Did you ever really take enough pills?

several of my therapists would ask later, when I managed to talk. No, I had not, and therefore, as they said, must not have been "in earnest."

Others would say, you see, your grandmother put up with infidelity, and perhaps your mother too: of course, you thought you had to. What was I doing now? Was this my heritage too?

We tried to resolve our problems. But didn't. Unable to stand it any longer, and after much going back and forth, I finally filed for divorce from the man I loved.

I needed help more and more. And less and less did I know where I could find it. I tried my church, Saint James Episcopal, on Madison, where I was assigned to the only woman priest. Sweet-faced and kind, she took me out for hot chocolate, mentioning that coffee was far too strong for her. That didn't bode well, I thought, since my problem seemed rather strong to me. She stared at me and my story and promised to consult her husband, who knew, she said, everything about cognitive psychotherapy. Yes, she would phone that night, certainly, with the name of someone I could see. She did not phone.

I phoned Peter, who said he could tell me whom to consult. Somehow, when he found the name of the man, that person didn't have time to see me. Nor did anyone suggested by various persons I asked. I was feeling increasingly desperate.

At last, an understanding friend gave me two names, both women. I made an appointment with the one who, said my friend, was used to dealing with high-powered people. I didn't feel very high-powered, but made an appointment anyway, and walked through the park to reach her. Dressed in some flowing thing down to the floor, in bright purple, she was listening to an opera on earphones, only one of which she removed to hear my story. I was reminded of Scottie my piano teacher, listening to things he preferred to my playing. I understood, but somehow this time, I felt unnerved.

This musical psychologist was savvy, amusing, sure of herself. And told me how she dealt with various opera singers, who would go out of their way to quarrel with their spouses or lovers just the day they needed their voices most, so that their throats would constrict and they could not sing. I was fascinated, flabbergasted. More so when she drew from me the information that while I was presiding over the Modern Language Association, I had had a strange number of breakfast quarrels with Peter just before having to chair some meeting or other. Perhaps I had done this on purpose, to punish myself. My eyes would be small and reddened, my voice hoarse: she was right.

But the next week, Mother was not well, and I had to cancel an appointment with the psychologist, to return to Wilmington.

You owe more to yourself than to her,

said she.
That did it. I never returned.

A week or so later, I tried the other woman, who began our first session with a command: "Tell me what are your goals." Goals: I didn't have those, or couldn't find them. Goals were not actually the point. Survival was.

Then I despaired of getting help, tried hospitals, tried referral services, wondered what I would have done without my job, my students, my friends. I knew how fortunate I was to be me, even a gravely depressed me.

Suddenly one day, walking miserably along Madison Avenue, just down from Seventy-ninth Street, I was halted by a sign reading: Short-Term Dynamic Psychotherapy. "Short-term": that sounded just right. I went up, filled out a "release" form before figuring out what the "release" was for. It was for videotaping, without which you could not return. When I inquired what this was about, they explained it was to confer with the team of experts.

Oh no, we don't release them to the public,

said the receptionist. I didn't feel reassured, but had no idea where to go next, so I acquiesced. A young man with a bright smile invited me to sit in the chair upon which the camera was trained. I saw no way out, and did. Within five minutes, I found myself weeping under his questioning. You see, he said?

You have lost all your personal pronouns, listen to you. You can't say "I" or "we" or "you." What are you going to do about this?

What was I going to do? I had no notion, and having asked this, he seemed not to have any positive ideas, having reduced me to tears. And said he was not sure they could help me, in my state. Then he left the room.

In came a kindly woman, who said she understood completely. She too was involved with a graduate school; she would love to make a series of appointments with me, at any time of the day. She seemed to mean it.

Seven in the morning?

I said, testing her. Fine, she said. Let me just ask you a few questions. Could the camera be turned off, I begged? Evidently not. This continued, with the lens trained on me. I have now no idea of her questions, my answers, or the point of it.

But to my horror, the young man returned, making a signal for the woman to withdraw.

You see, he said, you just have a problem dealing with men: you break down and cry when there is one of us around.
Would you like to see the tape, he asked? Or do you take my word for it?

I was speechless, and took his word for it.

Of those months, I remember nothing further now. It has made a black hole in my mind.

REALLY ALONE

So I was to be alone, in my city. I would walk to work down Park Avenue, where all the doctors' offices display their gold plates in the sun. The names

I was used to were now gone from the building I knew best, but my breath would catch there every time, with a sort of strange fear, I didn't know about what, but I could scarcely breathe. There in Dr. Equin Munnell's waiting room, all those years before, I had waited for news of the babies' coming. Waited in that low-key office, where you could read either the *New Yorker* or *Town and Country* with all the pictures of the well-groomed socialites I had been supposed to grow up into being. I had always looked wrong for that office, I felt. Always wrinkles in my tights at the ankle, my flat shoes with rubber on the bottom (arthritis, said the doctor, like your mother and sister, be careful), the color of my sweater too dull. Surrounded by all those other mothers-to-be, well garbed in their Armani suits, polished shoes, and Missoni sweaters.

Dr. Munnell, elegant and brusque, would look at me over his half-glasses and remark sternly upon my increasing weight. Like my father. I always felt awkward, inadequate, and heavy.

How it was for Hilary's birth. . . . I remembered Peter on the phone about some professional thing in the labor room, my mortification over the bloody sheets, over how little I was able to help myself with the shallow breathing I had gone up to this hospital to learn every week. I felt annoyed, pained, deceived; then being wheeled somewhere else, and then nothing. Except the glorious moment of seeing my daughter. Even my father, on the phone, sounded proud of me. It felt like spring, although it was December.

The second time, when Matthew was about to be born, it was late at night. I hadn't wanted to bother Dr. Munnell, in case those weren't real labor pains. I had waited far too long—especially for a breech birth. He had threatened a cesarian section, and Peg had come up to be with me. He scolded, as did the nurses and interns: did they have time to get me ready, how could I have done this, and so on. I was in pain, and felt truly wrong. I just hadn't wanted to bother anyone. Dammit.

The drugs can make you forget the pain,

said the doctor and nurses, in unison.

Nothing could lessen the pain I was feeling now, so many years later, walking by the scooped out building where Dr. Munnell's office had been. In my room, the answering machine, never turned off, kept its light steady. It had flickered less and less as the days went on. The little red light had replaced my husband. When I would lie down in half of my bed, I wouldn't even undo the spread. I'd leave the rest made up, while I myself took up less and less room.

If I don't talk to this self, no one will.

I am talking to myself, I say.

This was not the "I" that learned to speak in those pages I scribbled or typed in my journal like some dutiful schoolgirl, the ones that were supposed to show "improvement" after much anguish. These were not concerned with narration, with the outside real. In this dryness of love, in which I never wept, I felt nothing at all.

> *What is real is this. A nightmare, but imageless. A war rages and I think: it will finish this. I see doctors, lawyers, can't remember why, they too all wear wedding rings. How can you say what it's like to tear your wedding ring off? it is like killing a child. Not to have done that is not to have understood. I wore one for almost thirty years, and pulled it off. How to understand that?*

Someone reading this might say:

Yes, I understand. I mean, I haven't gone through it exactly, but I understand how it must be.

They may have a little smile of recognition.

Oh yes, I see.

What do they see? Nothing would appease this panic—this *emptiness*. I downed hot liquids: coffee, hot lemonade, tea, nothing filled that void inside.

But it is high time to pick up the pieces and try again. I set out every day now on my bike in Central Park, among the couples hand in hand, or bike by bike, and sit alone by the boat lake. There they are all coupled again.

I pedal slowly around the road, pushing hard to get to the lake on the other side, where we used to joke:

Oh, look, a lake!

This is where we solemnly buried the chicken Hilary had raised in her tiny slot of a bedroom, with Matthew in the other slot. The gerbil, Jennifer, when her feet got desiccated, was piped to her watery grave with Hilary's alto recorder. After the gerbil, some rabbits came on loan, leaving at their departure some tiny relics in the closet.

Oh look . . .

I am getting more eccentric by the minute. Losing my tickets to things, cluttering up my study with layers of announcements, misplacing the addresses I have filed here and there. Something joyful about chaos, though. It matches the mind. How can I be so happy and so chaotic? When I write, I lose my place, lose my file in the computer, have to start over many times. But it feels right, even as anyone else might think it peculiar: I am alone, I am aging, I am chaotic. And I am happy.

Miracles: I lost three student papers last week, and then found them yesterday. I feel frumpy: frumpy is OK, though. Have to remember that. I am still wearing coats far too large for me: I seem to need double protection. I have put an extra lining in on top of the wool lining, and still shiver a lot.

Last week it was time for my annual mammogram at the Guttmann Clinic. My university has an insurance program that lets you be x-rayed there free, and this is no time for me to incur heavy medical charges. The doctor says something may be wrong, please to wait for my report.

Not good. They have changed my number from 186100 to 186100A, they say on the first report. Now that seems, if a bit strange, all right to me. They assure me "it will make no difference to my report," due tomorrow. I have always been a trusting soul, maybe a trifle naive, but trusting.

Dear 186100,

says the report,

We are happy to inform you that the X-rays showed nothing to be alarmed about.

Right, but I wondered if I was still dear 186100, having been given the A at the end.

In some confusion and a lot of uncertainty—was my mind working?—I presented myself at yet another radiology center, where you could choose between a bright blue, bright yellow, or light blue examining smock. I hesitated for a longish time, torn between all three—no pink, no green, no white, nothing I dislike, all my three favorite colors in fact. And for some reason it seemed important, what I would choose. It was the bright blue. I made my way to the X-ray room, accompanied by a nurse who was plainly concerned about my getting yet another dose of X-ray.

I am just not sure, let us consult someone.

As I was about to take the X-ray, the radiologist also demurred:

Let us consult someone.

A kindly female doctor appeared, I explained my panic, and she sent me away un-x-rayed. Only I still worried. Whose X-ray was it anyway? I had brought with me, and seem to take them around from time to time, the previous pictures of my left breast, the one with the lumps. And now I wonder: will the next doctor recognize from the X-rays of 186100 (or is it 186100A?) on the right side that previous half of me?

Waiting for the report, I went alone to Serendipity—that palace of childlike delights across from Bloomingdale's where the frozen hot chocolate sets your mind at peace.

Party of one? asked the man in front.

What a horrible sound. How can you make a party of one? I loathe my self-pity. On WNCN the "Wedding March" was playing when I got back to my apartment. I turned it off, and tried humming something else to shut it out. I wanted to get back my energy; it had been long enough.

REAL HELP

Finally, after trying a number of therapists and psychoanalysts of all flavors, I asked my colleague Patrick for urgent help. He suggested a friend of his, a psychologist and writer, to whom I explained my deep unrest. Baylis knew how to get right to the heart of things, without delay. After I had been seeing him for a while, he tackled something crucial, that no one else had seemed to recognize as a problem. Certainly I hadn't.

One thing, says Baylis, that may matter for the future. Tell me about how you act in relation to authority. In your profession, I mean.

I am asked to do an interview with Jacqueline Lamba, the third wife of André Breton the surrealist, and a remarkable painter. I purchase a tape recorder and Peter and I drive to Simiane-la-Rotonde, a hilly town in the Vaucluse, to see her in an old castle-size mas, where our voices echo off the walls. She is astonishingly beautiful, and we strike up a friendship that will last; I sense it.

 A month later, after the four-hour interview, I transcribe it and send it to her. She writes back, in one of her four-color letters, that she doesn't speak well enough, not as well as André, and that I should erase the tape and tear up the script. I do so, even though I found it remarkable with its perspectives on Giacometti, Picasso, Artaud, and the surrealist scene. A week after that, I receive another letter that says it is all right, I may publish it after all, because she has granted an interview in Italy.

Why do I always and immediately acquiesce? I ask Baylis. Tell me more, he says.

 I write a Poètes d'aujourd'hui introduction to a French poet younger than Char, who has asked me to do it. Later, he asks the publisher to request I withdraw it, because he has found a famous man to write it; I cave in instantly.

 I translate Nathalie Sarraute's L'usage de la parole, working on it with her day after day, and then destroy it when the publisher who has commissioned it says someone else has translated the text and my work cannot be used.

This happens repeatedly in my professional career.

 I am putting together an anthology of essays on the avant-garde. Some of my more macho friends do not like being edited by a woman, as is suddenly apparent to me. One of them says to me, about the town in Sweden, "It is written Upsala, you know." No, I say, it is Uppsala, for instance, in the atlas. "Oh no," he says, "you are surely wrong." It is his article and he wants his spelling his own way. All right, I say. No one will know the difference anyway, and I would rather see a misspelling than have to confront a pride. Upsala it is. But in my stubborn mind, I know it is not.

What can I do about it? I ask Baylis.
What can I say to you? he responds. You have to work on yourself. You know that.

I know that.

Now I shut myself in a narrower and narrower radius; it is an effort to go outside, two blocks. Smaller and smaller, shutting myself in. Surrounding myself with objects, clothes, books—let no one get in here. This is just this. There is no narrative here. Nothing goes on. No one can hear what I am saying, when I really speak. Nighttime writing.
Will it always be this way, I wonder. Can anyone hear me?

Ah, Baylis might say, You were always lonely.

Or, with a gentle irony:

It is the fate of humans.

Maybe so. But for a while I thought not. I remember a blind girl at the only Saint Bart's singles party I ever attended, how she held out her hand, saying,

Hi, I'm blind.

She knew how to reach out. I have to try.

Five

The Alone Journals

Cambridge Journal

January 3, 1987

I HAVE BECOME A WANDERER. Too much pain at home.

I have come to Cambridge to get away. Clare Hall has invited me to spend the spring semester as a fellow. Peter has subpoenaed me and assured me that I can't really get away.

> They will follow you wherever you go: Cambridge, Oxford, they will follow you,

he said, of the legal papers, and I could feel my mind going. A totally irrational fear of the messenger, the law. I asked for this divorce, and cannot get my mind straight. The day I had to appear in court, my lawyer tried to help: take a walk, come look at these pictures, anything. The day was a blur.

I had to leave to see things in perspective, as I explained to Peg and the children. They all understood, and reassured me about themselves and myself.

> We'll be all right, Mummy, said Hilary.
>
> And we are here if you need us, said Matthew.

My mind was, is, in disarray. Yesterday, I just grabbed whatever clothes were on the right side of the closet, stuffed them into a suitcase while the subtenants, for whom I had not made out the proper papers, waited in the hall, picked up my portable computer, put on my heaviest coat, and got on the plane.

Here it was freezing, but anything is better than being where I was. I was going to weigh too heavily on the children, on my friends. What others in this position have done, I have no idea. I saw no choice, and left. But I had forgotten behind me in my apartment the instructions for the place I was to stay here in Cambridge, and had no idea what to do. I came, trusting in luck. At least, I am here.

I don't know where here is, here,

said my friend Jane Gallop in a lecture once. I don't either. But I arrived in Cambridge, shivering in my heavy coat, unsure, in the sleet and fog. By some miracle, Christopher, who teaches here, the only person I know, came weaving toward me on his bike, heading toward nearby Grafton Street where he lives. He made me tea and toast, got me settled. I miss Peg and the children.

February 15, 1987

Noise. That's what I have against Clare Hall, the noise of talk. I vastly prefer conversation, myself; but I expect you wouldn't know about that, being American.

This was Michael Jaffee, a well-known art historian, sitting across from me last night at dinner in King's, where I was Christopher's guest. Was I supposed to react? I tried a smile, and it stuck on my face; I could feel it. Not a sound came from my throat, not even the slightest noise. Christopher said something about what I had written, why I was here, to work on Bloomsbury things, and so on. But the voice continued, across the table, its accent perfect in its put-down:

They have to have wheelbarrows of publications, Americans—not a lot of quality, that's why.

Was this ordinary high table conversation? Was one to answer back? I couldn't, in any case. I have to learn to speak up, but it is slow going.

When I look out the window from the narrow house I have rented on City Street, the sign just across the way declares itself : "Thatcher's Poor." Downstairs is my ancient red bike on which I painted in white, that very first day, "Clare Hall 128." That was supposed to make it official, and less stealable.

There's no kickstand, so you have to lean it against walls everywhere. No Cycles, read the signs on the sides of buildings. Where was I to lean it? Such practical questions have begun to take over my mind. Good thing too.

At evensong, in King's College chapel, I sit almost every evening in the choir stalls near the choirboys chanting the antiphonal responses. Among the little boys on the front row, I like the one far shorter than the others, with large round glasses and an earnest face, probably up to some mischief or other. He often ducks down during the lessons to look out across under the stall and above the kneeling bench. He's the one I'd like to take home for tea, but of course, he always scampers off afterward with some older boys. Others are met by their families, older sisters in hair ribbons, parents smiling.

The life of learning and the life of family seem to follow two different paths here, that of the fellows, and the others: the hierarchical sense pervades everything, even now that the high table is usually on a level with the others, not raised as it used to be. The walks are divided into Scholars Walk and Family Walk, even here at Clare Hall, the most vigorously familial of all the colleges.

My wife can come in to dine even if I am not present,

said one fellow to me,

yes, she feels perfectly at home.

Well, I don't and, if anything, I'm scholarly. I am certainly not family now. Would I ever be again?

A letter from Matthew, in New York: "Oh my mother," he says, "rest in the green sereneness of England. A real boon." (I am using the word boon, he says, for the first and last time.)

March 7, 1987

The fens are low-lying, like marshes. Their name haunts me. The fens. Christopher took me one day last week to walk on the Roman Road: it was both chilly and warm, the road was a muddy slush. My feet kept emerging from my shoes, stuck firmly in the mud. His thin face intense, against the green splotches and the black earth.

It feels as if I am on loan. Christopher and the others seem to stand out in profile against the land they belong to, the institutions they are part of. I don't belong anywhere. The times I feel most myself are on bicycles, as if my biking in Central Park were carrying over. No one can get to your mind on a bike.

Biking takes a bit of practice here. I wobble my way just between the curb and the bollards, those iron posts upright in the middle of the walk. Whichever side you don't choose seems wider until you try it. Sometimes the bike basket won't go through the bollards. You have to get off, wedge the basket one way, then another, then leap back on, and off you go.

Every day, I have to make my way through these, down the little lanes behind City Street, over the green called Parker's Piece, past the Hobbs Pavilion, on to the main road. I cross at the zebra crossing, trusting the cars remember that bikers have the right of way, zip down the side street, holding out my arm to show where I am turning, repeat the process, thrust out the other arm, sometimes among great hordes of bikes. I lock up and take the batteries from the fixed lights, since they got stolen once during the dinner hour, and remove the portable ones.

A great string of bikers stride into the lecture room holding lights and notes. We bang down the wooden benches, exactly on the hour. If you get bored and leave, the bench bangs back up and everyone looks around. Late at night, returning on my bike, I go the way Christopher showed me, "easy as Bob's your uncle," pull the bike into the narrow corridor inside my front door, plunk down the ten books you can take from the library, and make my tea.

April 20, 1987

In libraries, I always feel I belong. Here I try to time it so I can have a hot cheese scone in the morning or a crisp flapjack in the afternoon. The air is steamy with the tea, and readers have that absorbed look they have nowhere else, except in the British Library Reading Room. The Bibliothèque Nationale has no such tearoom, and so it lacks that glorious feeling of the books awaiting you right overhead. You have to go out to a café. Forget I used to do that with Peter. Forget, forget.

In the enclosure of King's, leading to the library and archives, marked Members Only, the books reach to the ceiling. They look untouched since the last century, even though there are always students reading. In the back, up a small unmarked flight of stairs, are the modernist archives where I work. The librarian greets everyone like a special secret, because you have to sign up at least a month in advance, with the days you want to come. Your manuscripts or letters are laid out for you, and you feel guilty of a special affront if you cannot return when you are supposed to.

At lunch, I walk back to Clare Hall, often in a drizzle, along King's Walk, where the little flowers might be coming up soon. Over on the other side, sheep graze where there used to be cows.

But early morning is the best time. I saunter out in the chill, with all that expectancy about it, into the quiet streets: Fair Lane, Orchard Street, Paradise and Eden Streets, untouched since the last century. My jogging suit makes me feel serious about the morning. Out across Midsummer Commons, leading to Jesus Green, both by the river Cam, both a dull green against the gray sky. That's the memory I'll most want to keep. Like some Whistler colors, right to the heart. I stretch out one leg at a time atop the iron railings, and hold on. I grasp one leg and pull it up against me, then the other. This always feels like virtue itself.

All these weeks, right in the place where I do my first stretch, there has been a little heap of dog leaving, freezing over in the heavy cold, snow on it sometimes, then rainwashed. I wouldn't any more think of moving it or covering it over than changing my stretching place. No more than running on the cricket pitch in the center of all the green, even though it will be some time before they are out there, enacting their ritual. ("No American is really ever going to understand the game," they said, and you knew how very right they were. The foundation of British elegance, they said; right.) It may seem a bit slow, but slowing down is just what I need now.

May 8, 1987

When I walk by the river with Christopher, he covers up his face, pulls down his wool cap, and huddles in his torn parka like a leprechaun. The river is dull colored. We don't talk a lot.

The University Library is now filled at coffee time and teatime. I no longer feel a stranger. The various seminars prolong their discussions into drinks at the pub. Richard Rorty's Clark lectures on irony and the problems of liberalism are packed. I spend my time at Kettle's Yard, a sort of museum, and at the Fitzwilliam, often visiting its two small Constables in the upper gallery you reach by the narrow spiral stairs. Those clouds stay with you: "I have done some skying," he would write his friends. I think of the clouds over the Ventoux in the Vaucluse, and of Nicolas de Staël's clouds and sea.

The quiet of Cambridge has helped me come back to myself.

CALIFORNIA JOURNAL

September 2, 1989

Still wandering: not being attached has its advantages. I have been appointed as a Getty Scholar, to spend a year at the Center for the History of Art and the Humanities in Santa Monica.

On the way out to California, Peg joins me for a while. She and I travel through the arid lands of New Mexico. We are good traveling companions, silence and conversation in the right places for each other. Red land, black sky, the Taos Pueblo in the clear wind.

All the little sagebrushes are rolling into some furrows on each side of the road, which then close up.

What dreams I have, so many! I tell them to her, to remember them:

> We are joining the Hopi and the Zuni at a motel, taking the high and low roads at once.
>
> The walls of our living room at home are cracking, falling in: I am trying to put some pictures back on the wall before people come in to dinner. I stick them in the holes where they were, but all the frames are falling off.
>
> I am saying to Peter, who is wearing his tweed jacket with leather patches at the sleeves, "You'll always be my husband, sharing my Plato."
>
> I am dressed in black, and have become quite slim; I am simply leaving my family behind.

September 28, 1989

Good Lord. Why have I come here? I brought three pairs of sunglasses, and all I can see is that yellow mist ahead. What are they all smiling at, all these people in Santa Monica amid the palms overlooking the beach? Not pink and green shiny pants suits, like Florida, but lots of joggers, cyclists, walkers, runners.

Try not to notice when day drops away at five . . . it will happen at four, they say, just wait. When they set the clocks back. Set the clock back indeed: I couldn't even manage to turn off the alarm, that red dot stayed there.

When I push open the heavy iron-decorated door to the massive front hall of the house my apartment is in, The Embassy on Second Street, it is always dark, just the shiny covers of the magazines on the low tables gleaming with furniture polish, no one ever at the grand piano. It is utterly silent. In this old Spanish-style building, with the lush vegetation in front, past the overarching iron gate and the little white table with three chairs every which way, there always lingers a not unpleasant smell of insecticide, vaguely welcome and personalized.

My yellow secondhand bike has no gears and is a bit rusty, but it is a Raleigh and I love it. I enter the basement across the way where it is locked up, with a silver key that always has an air of magic about it, as I wait for the clank of the grill to open.

I trudge out along California Street to the ocean, overlooking the water with its paths impossible to get to unless you are good at carrying your bike down all those stairs or riding it past the pier, where it slopes down. Then you speed down alongside the cars and cut over in front of them, or ride down the sidewalk, getting off for anyone walking up. It's certainly not my familiar Central Park.

I ride every morning along the winding path by the sea, with the waves crashing distantly, the mountains behind them, and the endless homeless all about. One of them calls out:

How's it going, girl?
OK, I say, OK.

Somewhere, there is a sign for groceries, at the drab front of the One-Life Store. I pick up a carton of milk, put it in my denim knapsack on top of the sweater, and am about to set off again. Looming very tall, an unshaven man is standing in front of the wheels:

This is a boardwalk. Walk, it says: No Bikes.
Yes, all right,

I say, and wheel it off again.

Walk, he said; I said, boardwalk, and you are a bike.

How rapidly the light falls here. I push the bike along. In the dusk, wending my way home. I guess you learn to call anywhere you like just that.

October 6, 1989

California scenes, forever unlike what is inside me. A girl's long blond hair streaming out of the car window.

> *Home a long time ago, flooding back. Those mimosas heavy in the air, here too, the tiny petals fitting right into the little trefoil holes in the sidewalk. Yellow and pink roses everywhere, and along the palisades, white banana shrub. They had those by my house when I was little, where the rain would drum on the slate roof. . . . Stop and smell them, lie on the grass, no one minds. Walk over the concrete bridge, down the endless steps to the ocean level. Go down to feel the water: warm. Do I have time to go home, change, come back, swim? Should I work? Will this feel more familiar by June? Homesickness hovers unsurely in the bright air: no, I am not at home.*

Twilight seems not to exist here: or perhaps the ocean changes the nature of that long moment. One minute it would seem the perfect time for me to get my bike and bounce along the concrete to the little road down past the pier, in the admittedly waning sun, and the next, it would be almost nighttime.

If it was a little too dark to wind along by the ocean path, I would go out on the pier and have a few clams and maybe some white wine in a little paper cup outside in the back, on a shaky table, near the parking lot at Jack the Dragon's. Farther on, they were making fresh doughnuts, and the smell was comforting. I might even take a ride on the Ferris wheel, with its peculiar excitement.

I would spend hours walking along the pier, in the evening more even than in the morning. Pink and comforting, the cotton candy afterward would stick all along my fingers, even after being flattened by long sitting in its plastic bag in the dingy and deserted shop. I have a particular affection for cotton candy. I love to watch it spun about its paper cone from the enormous shiny round vat, the way I did when I was little, with my father at the circus. When Peter and I were first married, he gave me a small cotton candy maker, and a few bags of brightly colored sugar to use. . . . I remember wanting to save it, so I substituted less colorful sugar; when the machine finally broke, I still had most of the little bags of bright sugar.

I liked to stop before the fortune-teller Anessia, who would sit glowering at the passersby with her exhausted sister or her friend, generally in red, slumped over a chair by Anessia's sofa. Tonight the clown was in front, haranguing the strollers, while the live wooden Indian was clumping around. The saxophonist started wheedling away by the boathouse; the bikers were starting up the long climb of a path; the rows of lights around the carousel house were putting on their gaudy best; and it was time for me to wend my way back.

October 14, 1989

The best way to get the bike down to the beach is to cross on California Street, wheel it down the ramp while the cars spin by dizzyingly. You arrive at a cement ramp bridging over the road to the bike path. It goes along the sand, by the water, wending and winding its way under the pier, and then you roll ten minutes along to Venice, by the palms and the homeless drifters, with the water sparkling there, sometimes a sailboat. It feels like a great privilege. The tire is scraping against the fender, just a little, with a comforting sound, and I can hear my breath coming hard. The surf is slapping against the sand.

There is a comforting smell of onions cooking at the Rose Cafe, even in the morning. Every seat is taken outside under the umbrellas on the patio, the *New York Times* or the *Los Angeles Tribune* upon every table, cranberry nut or oatmeal or coconut muffins by the side, or perhaps the breakfast special: for $2.45, you get a croissant, coffee, and a substantial slice of Brie, butter, and jam. But I generally choose a foot-long cinnamon twist—crisp at the ends and just a bit sticky on the sides—they are heaped up, hot in an enormous basket, closely followed by the poppy seed croissants, puffy and glazed. There is a slight chill in the air, and all the tables except one are taken. And that is my favorite table, under the bottlebrush tree in the corner of the yard, by the bike racks.

A white parrot is perching on the shoulder of the girl laughing at the table in front of mine, which is half in the shadow.

> *I see myself having breakfasts alone in cafés everywhere: in London, in some Lyon's Corner House, or some ABC store, then some upmarket brasserie; in Paris, Le Rostand, across from the Luxembourg gardens, always the same long crusty croissants and the large cup of steaming coffee, with the little pitcher of frothy milk I would save and drink separately.*

And now the Rose Cafe in Venice, or the Cafe Casino in Santa Monica, with its *palmier* pastry and all the refills you like.

Coming back, you can go up Arcadia, toward the Appian Way, pushing uphill all the time. I cross over and use the bike path. Sun beating down now on my head. The Third Street market is in full swing: courgettes and mushrooms: girofles, chanterelles, and pleurottes; pistachios and dates, macadamia nuts, fresh basil, cilantro, and tiny eggplant to sauté in garlic and very green olive oil, with tomatoes and some Monterey Jack, and then cover with fresh basil . . . okra in large pods and very tough—I just suck out the insides; honeys of all descriptions, beans and peas by the dozen kinds and shapes and prices, and lettuces, crinkly and smooth . . . tiny yellow and red peppers, and even four kinds of home-baked pies.

Everyone around is as brightly colored as the market. I am mostly in gray, or something black, but they are all in pink and green, purple, yellow. Chatting and laughing, holding up the herbs to the sun. Comparing the mushrooms.

October 16, 1989

There is a circus tent on the beach: go see what's up. Have some clams and come back. Tears stinging my eyes over the acrobats falling so bravely into the nets. Speak of projection! The crowd loves this clown, who asks with his sad face if I am from Australia.

No, I'm not.

So then what are you doing here?

continues the clown.

I don't really know, I say.

At the Getty Center, all the scholars there for the year head in for afternoon tea. (The theme this year is the avant-garde: I'm working on John Ruskin, as well as Robert Motherwell and Joseph Cornell. I don't feel very avant-garde to me. Maybe I got selected—to my surprise—because I'm translating Jacques Derrida's book on the portraits and writings of Antonin Artaud?) I love in particular those crunchy Bordeaux cookies made by Pepperidge Farm. I am convinced I write anything better after them. When I was writing poetry, years ago, it was the thick taste of a milkshake and the sight of the drops condensing on the outside of the cold metal container they beat it up in. The way the traces would still mark the inside when some was poured out. Once I broke one of my front teeth in an eager encounter with a pecan pie. This is not what you would call a sophisticated attitude at teatime.

I often start the day with a spoonful of ginger marmalade, preserves, really. The morning glory makes a fence of blue as I trundle my way to my office to write, after biking back from breakfast. I go past the guard, always smiling, past the yellow flowers tall in a massive vase: when I stop to sniff them, the other passersby stare. I suppose they are used to flowers. In general, I don't get used to things.

December 12, 1989

Out in the early Sunday light, before the cyclists clog the beach path and the joggers, the paths under the palms. Today, I am walking. . . . In my right pocket, the ten quarters I had saved all week to buy the *New York Times* from one of the row of machines, but they are all yesterday's.

I make my way slowly past the twenty or thirty homeless to the Santa Monica pier, out over the water. Between the bare wood of the pier slats, you can see the waves: like those of the pier in the little beach town where Peg and I grew up, in the summers, and where we still walk when I go home, to the inlet far up the beach, and out on that pier, to sit on the high benches with some coffee, looking out to sea. Here, as I look down, the rough water is framed by the splintering boards, far below yet dizzyingly near. Some days I can only look at the smallest things: the grain of the wood, the particular green of the sea.

Coming back from the ocean walk, I bury my nose in the dark green roughness of the cedar trees. Then in the tiny white flowers by the restaurant Fennel, and later in the magnolia blossoms in my courtyard.

Home: here in the courtyard, the shadows cast by the shrubbery are sharp angled, marking the special chill of the coming evening after the ardent day. Coming home. Every time you have to fill out forms, even for a bike lock, the question is what is the name of someone who will always know where you are. . . . Who would that be, I wonder.

It is a lot harder being alone than people say. I think they don't know.

January 20, 1990

At the San Vincente Salon, where I go for evening exercise classes, at least one-third of the class look like Michelle Pfeiffer, who comes here to exercise. Radiant faces on all sides; confidence everywhere.

> I'll give you an easy elastic,

says the exercise instructor. She is lissome, brown, in perfect shape with pink undergarments showing under the tight white cotton shorts. She smiles at me in a kindly manner.

We slide the bands over our ankles to step side to side, eight to the right, eight to the left, hobble hobble hobble. A sort of conspiracy between the older exercisers—surreptitious glances to see who gets tired from what, and how soon.

The jargon of exercise classes:

> tempo now, let it drop, hustle forward, hustle back, isometric right here . . .

My mind wanders to isomorphs . . .

> Ladies, wake up.

We pick up weights: I choose the lightest, and the instructor smiles sweetly at me.

My knee hurts: I'll have to take care of it.

> How you doing, girls?
> Swell,

they all say.

At the café afterward, women in red jogging outfits are everywhere, around me, behind me, beside me; the chatter continues.

> My nephew is reading Rimbaud, he got through Mallarmé. Want another bite?

Across from me, in the light through the trees: two elderly blondified women, comparing dictionaries and lists.

> Did you hear me use exacerbate? Remember yesterday I used titillate? Now I could have said: exaggerate. Shall we try another?
> Let's try another, yes.

Two other high-pitched voices:

> Have you noticed in the dancing class all the bodies in shape?
> Yeah, much better figures. In aerobics, they just let go.

Heavens: and me, I'm about to let aerobics go, since my awkwardness is intense. The young instructor with her perfect figure in her perfectly hued outfit exudes cheer every session:

> See how simple. Two steps right, two left, grapevine right, grapevine left, hustle forward, knee high, hustle back, grapevine right, grapevine left, how are you feeling?

And smiles encouragingly.

I smile back, expecting I look pretty wan. *I hate this.* On either side of me, young things in their pale pinks and pale blues.

> Go on home, says the instructor.
> Home base, Mother would say This is home base.

The colors of the countryside around that home were tender and eye-stinging. The misty gray and green of the inland waterway where those white boats would move so slowly, going under the bridge with their masts high. The bridge would lift, and we would laugh with delight, Peg and I.

March 23, 1990

Things seem calmer when I am running, creeping really, along the Palisades, strained faces on each side of me, with the water glinting in the distance. Or biking all around, with the reward of sitting in the café afterward—but that stone in my heart.

At least I am not wearing dark glasses now.

Salad bars seem very wilted at night, but that is what I have been living on for months. I go at eleven at night.

This will have been your life,

Patrick used to say in his low tones. This is what you will have had. He was never given to optimism.

Are you doing your best?

that is what I always asked my children to do, just their best, for them.

That is asking too much, said Matthew.
OK, said Hilary with her quiet smile, I will.

With Pat Terry, my poet friend here in California, with whom I love to translate, talk, and travel, I purchased a black leather jacket a few weeks ago, to look New York tough. I hoped it was right for listening unobtrusively to Matthew's band, and showed him:

Just right, he said.

May 3, 1990

I wake with a start. How could I not have seen this before. I have come out here, and everything I love is back there. My family, my memories, my friends, my colleagues. Carolyn, Gerhard, Patrick, all in New York, Matthew nearby, Peg and Sarah Bird in North Carolina, Hilary and Jonathan upstate. I suddenly see them all afresh. How grateful I am.

Where have I been in my mind? But my mind is better, wherever it has been. Grateful is exactly what I am.

New York and Elsewhere, Alone

June 15, 1990

Another great day in the Metro,

says a loud voice behind me. I and hundreds of others are riding up the escalator at Dupont Circle in Washington, D.C., taking a long vertical tunnel toward an oval of sky, with slants of bright rain, like that Braque painting in the Phillips Gallery with its bicycle leaning against the tree and the silver streaks aslant.

Back to the Archives of American Art, where I had gone to pore over some books Joseph Cornell used to own. But I can't see very well, and I squint hard, wrinkling up my nose, which is supposed to convince me I am seeing better. To my astonishment, the custodian reaches in her desk to bring out her own pair of magnifying half-glasses:

Here are some eyes for you, she says.

"Some eyes for me." I'm learning how to accept things, little by little. I have to combat that whole refusal stance of my family: never staying more than one day with anyone—"we don't want to put them out." I am delighted to have these other eyes.

In the evening, I go to the Kramerbooks and Afterwords café, to meet Roxana, my former student. Blond and vigorous, she comes along swinging her arms, with a tremendous smile:

I want to hear about you.

Solidly, she is there, supportively: she never gives you the feeling I have so often given myself and others, of being about to go. Some idea I've inherited of never staying anywhere: as if staying were always to impose oneself on people and their places. What if I weren't a burden, can I imagine that—someone people would like to see, and see more of?

When I was growing up, teachers were always the ones who helped, urged, were to be counted on. Now I know it works the other way also. Roxana says:

> Go on, please go on. How are you doing? What are you doing for yourself? I want to hear.

At the next table, the snazzily dressed young lady is saying to her serious young man with leather patches on his subdued heather tweed,

> Washington's so much nicer than Paris.

Looking deeply into her eyes, the young man replies:

> You don't have to choose between them. They're both fine cities.

Roxana and I smile across the table at each other at such banalities, but which of us doesn't fall into them, all the time? God, am I lucky to have my students and friends. To have people to pull me through, and to let me help them pull through whatever they most dread.

November 13, 1990, Woodstock, New York

Matthew and I have come here, three hours away by bus; we each take a window. We've come to try cross-country skiing for the first time, as we have promised each other for years. It has rained on the snow, and so we just walk, me in his boots over two pairs of socks—we stride about in the white expanse, and sit talking on the black logs, by a rapid river just as black.

We remember walking up part of the large pyramid Cheops together in Egypt, after dinner in the Meena House, with searchlights trained on us—and talking there, with our backs against the slope of the side. Newly divorced, I was feeling my way again with everyone, even the children. "This marks a new point in my life," said Matthew.

I left my glasses on the bus coming back. I keep leaving my glasses everywhere these days, in restaurants and at people's houses. Maybe there are things I'd rather not see. Specious psychologizing, probably. Especially since

I often leave things: my talks I've been preparing with such excitement, in the pocket of the plane seat going over to Paris, where I tend to leave my glasses too. Take it as unimportant, and get on with things, I say to Matthew—that's what I have to do. When his favorite guitar was stolen, he had to do that too.

October 21, 1991

Work on spunk. Have spunk. I get some new glasses, and when they are being fitted I try to hold my chin up higher than usual, so that I'll have to do that to see.

Breathing: I am being taught new things about it in a smallish class at Miss Gefühl's West Side apartment. We are breathing through a straw, letting the air out little by little. You are supposed to notice "what happens in your body." I am not sure anything is happening at all in my body. More in my mind. But every bit of slowing down is good, like the Zen sitting techniques I'm also trying. I've lived things so rapidly: work, talks, teaching, friends.

Around me, several large Viennese ladies in hairnets are wearing sleeveless white leotards, as Miss Gefühl has requested:

I can watch the muscles better, she says, radiant in her self-assurance.

My leotard is black. If I had any muscles, I don't think she could see them. I don't know if I have any at all.

This is intensely boring. After a very long hour and a half, we are permitted a small movement of a leg or an arm, to ascertain how we control ourselves in slow motion. Then we all stand in a little cluster and gently pat the back of the person in the center of the huddle. The others clearly enjoy it. I just feel ganged up on.

Then we lift ourselves up on our thumbs for support, to realign our vertebrae. It is all done with high drama.

See how much progress you are making!

Miss Gefühl shouts. Her wrinkled face beams at us, for she knows her system works. Only if you believe in it, though. Hard to believe in other people's systems, when all mine felt such failures. The unhinging of the self, someone said to me. How to rehinge . . .

November 2, 1991

Walking in the park today with Carolyn, who loves the cold. Not me. She has lost a scarf, and finds it.

> A good sign, I say.

She smiles at me. I'm always seeing signs in everything. It's like wishing on everything: the first evening star, the first slice of lemon in your teacup, the first day of every month. I used to wish, when I was little, that no one would be hungry and everyone would be happy.

We stop for her to pet every dog, to feed the horses carrots. We will always walk together, when we can; We can talk about everything. We walk slowly, arguing about what matters in poetry, each convinced we are correct, and decide we both are. Alone, I dash along, as if I had always some place to get to. How to slow down?

Thanksgiving Vacation, 1991, Saint Thomas, Tortola, Virgin Gorda

Off on a group sail, got to get over loneliness. Delayed at the airport; the leader of our group complains about the anguish this is causing him. His forehead goes bright red:

> Our whole vacation is ruined. They will pay for this.

I'm embarrassed, hate loud talking. Sitting quietly across from us, an elegant shabby early-elderly couple. Are they a couple? His eyes blue in a tanned face, under gray brows and a cap. His tweed jacket brown-green and his tan cord trousers, the kind that go well with a camel jacket, exude the same atmosphere and sporty smell as the squash racket in its green bag with the blue trim. He will not be raising his voice, even if we miss four planes. Peter would not have complained either. Would have made some witty remark. They will be traveling lightly, and elegantly, wherever they go.

His eyes twinkle when he looks at the woman by his side. Her gray hair is neat, with a blue tinge to it above her horn-rimmed glasses; her feet are shod in elegant narrow gray shoes of soft leather. Her gray duffel bag with its red handles just matches the spirit of his green one with its blue trim. All very J. Press or L. L. Bean or Land's End, probably the latter. They must have weathered a lot together: loss of friends, maybe some disappointment or ex-hilaration over their children.

Now on the plane they are sharing a magazine—that is what I long for. The kind of life I suppose I thought I would have. Well, maybe I do: Patrick and I sharing coffee, books, CDs. My colleague Gerhard, and I having brunch every week. Nothing turns out the way you think.

After a few transfers, we are finally on a large ferry, heading for our boat. Out the window: a blond young lady, blue-eyed, very short black skirt and a black and white top, with a deprecating smile, asks the ferry be pulled back in for her—it is done, the little runway is thrown back over to land, the green platform is put down once more, the anchor is tied again. She smiles and trips aboard. How do you learn that self-confidence?

On the boat, I go up early on the deck to read when things are quiet. The small sound of the water lapping against the side of the boat. Under sail, a gull sways left and right ahead of the boat. The clouds stream down into the sea.

Now the black clouds are passing over the pink, as I take a walk on the beach. A tire has been left dangling, to swing from, so I do. A few vacation-ers walk by, smile at me there, a girl no more, swinging all the same.

In West End, Tortola, some cocks are crowing. Day is breaking quietly. Later, somewhere else in this sparkling expanse, we go snorkeling over schools of bright fish, corals, a wrecked ship, the bubbles of the scuba divers floating up in crystal circles, like swimming in champagne.

Under way now again, heading off wind, downwind. I am supposed to do the sailing, out here, off the far reefs. I feel squeamish about it.

You have done harder things,

says one of my sailing companions. Don't know how he knows, but he's right.

December 5, 1991

At vespers tonight, where I went with Gerhard, there was Patrick, sur-rounded by his adoring students ("scholarettes," he calls them), his delight showing. In his blue blazer and chinos (this is December, but he never gets cold)—how I love his face.

I love you,

to whom else could I say that so openly now? Like a brother, I add in my mind, so that I will remember I know that.

I've been doing too much jogging. My left knee is worse, my right big toe too: *rigidus halidus,* says the doctor. Better put a spike in that shoe so it won't bend. Sounds terrible, feels worse. I won't do it. I am only comfortable in running shoes. All my women colleagues here wear elegant high heels, besides speaking perfect French and keeping up with the world, as they had at Barnard.

January 1992

In am in Key West for my first "writers' conference" and I believe it will be my last. I just came to be with Sarah Bird, who is amused by them, but that's because she does travel writing on the side.

I can't take it all in,

says a lady of great girth, her pleasant face wreathed in smiles.

I saw three celebrities last night. How many are you up to?

At Hemingway's house with the large porches and the six-toed cats, I see in a display case *Essays Old and New,* edited by Essie Chamberlain, with its familiar faded green cover, a diagonal stripe running across. On the lawn, late afternoons in Washington, at National Cathedral, I used to read, longing for something indefinable, thinking it might be in those pages somewhere. In comes the guide with her high-pitched troop of wide-eyed gigglers, and I flee.

The revival churches with their doors open, hymns coming out in waves, washing over me as I lean my bike wheel against the curb. A dog barks and tries to nip at my trouser legs as I pedal off. The bougainvillea, the twisted vines hanging from the trees. The long vines we swung on at our school, Forest Hills. No hills were ever in sight, and the forest is long since gone.

No one is in a hurry in Key West,

says a man passing by, and smiles at me on the bike I have rented for the day, in order to see the Casa Marina where Stevens stayed and the White Pier where—according to the guide—Robert Frost and Tennessee Williams read aloud "The Idea of Order at Key West." Maybe.

On the spur of the moment, I plop down a check to go snorkeling.

At a reception last night for the "visiting writers," I asked Calvin Trillin, while I was struggling with a cold and clammy conch beignet, where and what to eat: I knew he would know, and thought he might not mind being asked. He didn't. Oysters at Pepe's, he responded. I love the name of those oysters: Apalachicola.

Another night, Sarah Bird and I went to find some crabs, and had them peppery and steamed—laughing over the shells and strewn parts around us on the newspaper, gesturing at each other, mallet in hand.

January 24, 1992

A heap of clothes Peter left behind emerge from under a pile of sweaters in the closet. A rough black cotton shirt from Mexico, a pair of swimming trunks, his school tie with purple stripes I used to like. I bundle them up, take them to my office, and send them to his secretary. No tears this time.

Lives change, I say aloud to myself.

That sounds convincing. Perhaps I will be convinced.

This is one of those overcast, expectant Sunday mornings in my city. Other bikes jamming into mine in the crammed basement—the joy of extracting it, wedging the basket out between the others. Picking up the paper, dumping out sections: business, sports, real estate, and want ads, a pound less in the basket. The park is cold, traces of snow.

Past Dog Hill, where we used to sled with the children. Quiet this early, in the gray air. My tires go haltingly over the bare earth with all its roots sticking up, over the pitted asphalt, to the boathouse like another home. I have a heated bran muffin and coffee. The tables overlooking the lake are now black iron and large, instead of the spindly white iron ones that used to scrape across the floor.

Riding slowly amid the runners with strained faces, I recognize some from my times jogging around the reservoir. The implicit bonding when we would do our stretching exercises on the little iron bridge after going around. Now at the fallen jogger's memorial, the hand-lettered sign is gone. Two police cars are parked across the way. A simple pot of fresh flowers marks the place she was attacked.

This afternoon, I'll walk with Carolyn again: she will be bundled up, like me. Maybe she will feed the horses. I know she'll stop to speak with all the dogs.

February 20, 1992

Patrick knows about music like Matthew does. I feel at home in his apartment: an expanse of wood floor with worn Persian carpet and a harpsichord at the far end, neat rows of compact disks lining the hall, books up to the ceiling all around. One friendly gray cat is curled up on his worn briefcase; a fiercer one—or more timid—resides in the kitchen, next to thirteen umbrellas all the same taking up the wine rack. Vitamins and kelp take up the fridge; when we stayed in London together once, he persuaded me to drink some of the foul green stuff. It or something has kept him looking very young. We go to concerts and plays and museums together, always at ease, brother and sister. Like being with Gerhard.

How little you want,

says Gerhard's therapist to him. And tells him a story he then tells me:

You get to heaven, and God says: Just look at all this. I want to reward you. Choose anything. Take anything you want, anything. And you say: Could I have a roll? and you hesitate: With perhaps some butter?

October 9, 1992

I had been waiting to see the Matisse show at MOMA, my ticket carefully put aside. Maybe not so carefully; it was for the first hour this morning. Nowhere to be found. Don't condemn myself.

At the Met, the Glenn Gould films again. His ecstatic face, hunched over the keyboard, for the Goldberg Variations. The way he sings to himself and conducts, circles with his body, throws his head back. Held forever on film; he will not age for us. That last variation, so quiet you hold your breath. Things we can keep.

Tomorrow is Sunday; I'll take a ride in the park. Then go walking with Carolyn: this time I'll take the carrots for the horses.

Rehinging.

October 10, 1992

This early morning Sunday I ride my bike slowly up the hill to Guy Pascal's, settle down with the *Times* at my favorite corner table, order an almond croissant and a little pot of coffee. At the next table, my neighbors grin at me.

In the arts section, Faye Dunaway, bless her heart, is speaking of the difficulties of being an aging film actress and wanting a role where, she says, she can be who she is. "I want to play real women, authentic, feeling, vulnerable, tragic, funny women." Sounds good to me. Those are the parts I want to play too. Though I could do without the tragic. Maybe that's a choice I can make for the future.

On the other side of the park I stop by a tree overlooking the lake way below, choosing a place to sit on a large piece of bark torn off in the recent storm. The colors of autumn—the haze is golden around the two gaslights left on; a jogger is reflected in the lake, her legs moving as in a silent film above her head. What quiet: take it with me.

At home, a message: Carolyn has an extra ticket for the Matisse show: can I go at twelve? I think of Bernard in *The Waves,* losing his ticket, finding his ticket. I like Carolyn's finding mine for me. Sometimes you find what you lose; sometimes you have help. Excited, afraid I'm late, I bang the door shut on my finger, rush back in to wash the wound and put Band-Aids all over it, and dash out the door again.

At the exhibition I look for a long time at Matisse's *Window at Collioure,* one of those views opening out to the sea, crammed with the masts of sailboats, some greenery just above them; pink, the whole thing gloriously pink. There are worse things than filling up a space with pink. My finger is throbbing, should have taken more drastic measures. Proust's Bergotte, going from his sick bed to see the little stretch of yellow wall in a Vermeer, art and death. What an inappropriate comparison, one part of my mind says. OK, says the other, but that's what my space is filled with. Use what you have.

At home again: Matthew has left me some gauze and tape for my finger. And a note: "Take care of yourself, Mummy."

October 30, 1992

A feminist conference celebrating my friend Carolyn: "Out of the Academy, into the World, with Carolyn Heilbrun." I am to introduce her as the main speaker, and, doing that, I forget to introduce myself. They've all said their names, except me. Doesn't matter. We all wear T-shirts with Carolyn's and Amanda Cross's books listed on them, the name on her detective stories. Susan Heath comes up, such a nice face:

> Remember me? I'm the person who asked you, some years ago, what you were going to do with all that anger you have inside you? You didn't answer then. I think you're answering me now,

she says. I feel encouraged. I do remember; the whole thing comes back.

> I'm still learning,

I say.

It feels like getting back in touch with something I almost lost. But it's not anger, it's me.

"Rage begins at home," I thought, having known what it was to have an angry father, an angry poet, and an angry husband. All for different reasons, with different ways of showing it, but I did wonder. Might it be that some early acquaintance with it leads you to seek it out later? Marrying Peter, I thought I was seeking brilliance, someone I could look up to, but perhaps I was seeking what I had always known.

> What do you know about it?

my father would ask Peg and me, whatever opinion we were venturing. Sure enough, we felt we knew less and less about whatever it was. Knowing less, we felt more.

And then, after Peter, there was my poet, René Char, massive and full of angry temperament. He was cosmically angry. Knowing him for so long, and then having moved my family to be near him, I realized I was spending quite a bit of my adult life, as I had my child's life, in tears, unable to speak, for someone else's rage. I translated his poetry, wrote three books on him, and loved him. We all did. He was in himself a universe, unforgiving, believing himself kin to the constellation Orion. We would all go out under the Vaucluse sky to see his constellation, and knew ourselves fortunate to live in his proximity. I never got over loving this raging poet, as much for his rage, as for his language.

But when I felt it was time for me to write on someone else, he raged as he never had before in my presence:

You will write on little poets, will you?

His rage must have reached me. I remember bursting into tears, there in his study, he sitting on his green sofa and me standing, weeping only out of one eye, ludicrous and fully conscious of it, raging against myself for my weakness. One-eyed weeper trying to say something. I hurled the sheaf of papers I had for yet another book on his work across his desk. He did not improve the matter by his response:

You, you have always been presence for me. The others are just absence. Colorless.

I continued weeping, as if in some intellectualized rape scene.

I have not learned anger completely enough, and do not even know if I am still weeping inside. I think perhaps so. My poet is dead, my father is dead, my marriage is broken—"these bonds," we once said to each other, "are of bronze and cannot be broken"—but they are. Is it now my anger I muster, now that I weep no longer outside, or is it something else?

I can, however, tell you what I suspect it is. It is an energy nourished by the rage that will not speak its name. Some things southern females do not learn how to speak out about. I have lost all those three males, each in a separate time, and each was full of anger—and I have gained something I am learning to call myself.

Why am I so often at a loss for words? I see back now: I am elected to the Modern Language Association council for the first time. Germaine Brée, generous and the MLA's president that year, wants to get me to talk. "We have not yet heard Mary Ann," she says. And indeed they would never have, nor would I have heard my own voice saying anything, had she not asked.

So someone had to make explicit room for me. I had to be invited to speak, for I had lost my words, and could not state my reason or my anger at— whom?—myself. I am above all angered at having been angry at myself. This is a learned self-chastisement, surely, a Protestant, even Episcopalian reaction, and I am angry at it. At least I can use that anger as the starting point for the rest, as a white-hot beginning, should I want to start over. I want my past rage against my own past inability to speak to count now. I want its intensity to pervade what I write, live, say. I want to bear witness to how the personal heat of it can burn out any vestige of the numbness of heart—in myself or others—responsible for so much. "Taking the heat," this is called; well, I want to take the heat into my writing.

I've asked my students to write something personal. One of them begins: "It's hard to learn to be me. But I'm catching up." Me too. Hilary caught up with herself long ago: so much she could teach me. As Peg says of her, she may well have been the "the one 'found' person in our family." She knew who she was and moved toward what she was sure of, knew what was important to her and stayed faithful.

November 12, 1992

Rushing from my office to the Museum of Modern Art for an early Godard film, I feel my pantyhose descending around my heels. I stop in at Saks, take the escalator to the ladies room, pull them up, tie a knot in the elastic at the waist and set out again. Halfway there, up Fifth Avenue, they are dropping again, so I stretch out my legs as far as I can on each side to hold them up, as I grab at them through my coat and skirt on one side. The last time this happened, it was summer, and my skirt was linen, so I could reach through it a lot better.

Last night, a glorious two-part concert at the Miller Theatre at Columbia: Complete Cello and Piano Works of Beethoven. Two members of the Juilliard String Quartet, Joel Krosnick and Gilbert Kalish. Matthew with me to the first part, sesame noodles and hot and sour soup together at Ollie's, across the street, and then alone to the second part, beginning with the Sonata in A Major. The cello part stays with me. If I could play an instrument, that is the one I would choose.

FIXING ME UP

Some of my friends are trying to fix me up with somebody. They keep finding some staid type with a paisley tie, his shoes just polished, saying he is delighted to take me to tea. Now nobody knows better than me—I've taken out British citizenship after all—what it's like to spend a truly invigorating afternoon at the English Speaking Union over a nice cup of Earl Grey with maybe a cucumber sandwich and a shortbread biscuit if you're lucky. You poise yourself on a chintz-covered chair, flip through the pages of the *Independent* or the *Observer* for a real treat, and are on your best behavior. Ten to twenty minutes of discreet conversation about the weather in Scotland, though, can get you down.

Tonight my English department colleague Fred and his wife, Evelyn, as deeply New York as Peter is deeply English, wanted to have a little chat with me at their house over dinner. What I need, they say, is my opposite. So what I should do is read the personal columns in some journal like *New York* or the *New York Review of Books* and respond. While Evelyn prepared dinner, Fred gave me a pep talk.

No way, I said, no way. Could I have some more wine please?

To get me in the mood, Fred showed me some back issues. His favorite goes:

Monteverdi lover, jazz musician. Six feet four, plays a mean trumpet, swinging personality, loves Bechet and Bach, sings to any tune. Let's make music together.

That's one for you, says Fred, how about it? You could make music together, Mary Ann, how can you resist? I glare. He continues:

Married man invalid wife desires submissive female with interest in S/M etc.

And then:

Virile gentle computer expert desires young thin redhead for exciting travel.

Oh great, I say to Fred, I get it, you want me to put in something like:

Brilliant single blonde with perfect figure wants to meet like-minded and like-shaped man of 35–45 for jivey life style.

Fred goes glum. I know he's trying hard, so I try to take it seriously. If you can't take your friends seriously, you've had it. We find one for me, and I promise I will answer:

Mathematician, very bright, interested in everything. Professor and writer, would like to meet teacher and writer.

OK I will try. I take down the box number and write a note.

The math man phoned to meet me, at my beloved boathouse in Central Park, after my class in modern poetry. It was a disaster. I phoned Fred to tell him all about it. There he was, I told him, in bright red trousers. I had put on my cheeriest outfit, feeling like a peppermint stick in my pink jeans and lighter pink T-shirt. We had coffee and a very large chocolate chip cookie broken in two. I did my best, tried to concentrate, smiled, nodded. (Spoke, did I speak?)

You are not listening to me,

said the red trousers. I had had to admit that he had some justification there. It was mortifying:

I am telling you I read Henry James too,

he said,

and I love *The Divine Comedy,* and you can't even hear me.

I was mortified, caught up short in my snobbish past and my pink jeans, and at a loss. I apologized and we parted. I was completely in the wrong, end of story, I said to Fred. I see, he said. I expect he was not surprised.

The next day, Evelyn phoned. She isn't one to give up, even if I am. Let me read you something, she said:

> Affectionate romantic
> Jim McMullen's dinner
> Spencer Tracy look-alike
> Call me hurry

Jim McMullen's isn't far from you, said Evelyn, so answer. Try. For me. I did.

Well, hello there,

says Spencer Tracy on the phone,

Hello, honeybee! I can sense your pheromones!

Puh-leese . . . of course I was too embarrassed to hang up. Jim McMullen's because he's Irish, he had said. So I went. It was unforgettably awful. McMullen's we tried, with lots of young preppies waiting around.

Always bring my new dates here,

said Spencer Tracy to me. Terrific, I thought, I'm just loving this. But luckily, there were too many people there for him, so we tried another place: he had three Dewars, one after the other.

We are just getting to know each other,

he said to the waitress. So we couldn't order and get it over with.

So you are not to bring any food until I finish my whisky, OK, cutie?

I waited it out during the three Dewars. Then came the unbearable part: he wanted to say grace before the meal. Right here.

The Lord is my companion in everything. You know.
Sure,

I said, taking the freckled hands he stretched out across the Dewars and my
white wine, just as the mussels marinara finally appeared.

Feel better than ever. I can tell the Lord is always with me. Don't you
feel Him here with us?

I felt nothing at all but a desire to leave. A little later, he pointed out that he
rode a bike just like me,

and not one of those things with gears, nope, a coaster bike, Columbia,
the kind my father had. Hard to get.

Finally it ends. I have done my part. Amen.

A technicality, who makes the move to end it, said Baylis. Am I stating
the obvious?

Not a lot of things are obvious to me. I'm never sure what year what
happened or what is happening now, anywhere, or ever did, which forms to
throw away from the bulging folders I can't close. He's right: some of my
relationships have ended other ways, but all seem to end.

You're weird, you're really weird,

says one friend. But I felt increasingly OK. Not so weird; I am just driven.
I want to write.

I have too much to do, accept too many commitments.

Learn to say: f—— off. Can't manage it? How about just "stuff it"?

Gerhard is my favorite colleague, and I often see the reasons. We have
brunch in Squid Roe (half carafes of screwdrivers and mimosas, bluefish and
scrod), espresso afterward at Cafe Bianco. No strain, why isn't everyone like
this? Just as Matthew would say, over our pikilia and retsina at the Greek
Village,

Why can't you say to yourself, "Just stop. Stop right here."

On my wall Matthew had taped:

Tell them NO!
"I'm recovering.
I shouldn't work.
Sorry.
Good Night."

I am at the Met, standing again in front of the Ryder painting Toilers of the Sea *with its sailboat and black sea, its sun with the ring around it, its cracked surface surviving from the 1880s, and his* Moonlight Marine, *with the uneven densities of its pain.*

I have been seeing Joshua, a professor of linguistics at Columbia, who speaks what seems like every language under the sun.

If we are together fifty years, he says, smiling in his gray beard, I will never bore you. I promise you that.

I guess it's arrogant, I can't tell. An Old World type. He walks slowly, savoring each minute, waits for me, phones every day to worry about my rushing around. He's right, of course. I always take on too much.

One year, I went down to Princeton every week to hold a seminar. I would leave my slides behind, take the wrong ones, become exhausted, as I was directing the doctoral program in comparative literature at my own graduate school at the time. Another time, just before leaving for France, I taught a semester at the School of Visual Arts: I felt drained, by the studio visits, by the large class, by their enthusiasms, so different from my own. Keep my own enthusiasm intact. Figure out how to do that.

I'm struck by Joshua's neatness, his shoes tidy on the polished floor. He seems turned toward an interior and a past: all the yellowed pictures on the walls, all the albums with pictures of his former wives and girlfriends. He is methodical and patient with himself, the opposite of me, always wanting to do everything at once: make the artichokes and the bouillon with light cream and fresh basil for all those people arriving for dinner, write another chapter, set off on my bike all at the same time.

It will never work, says Sarah Bird, about my relationship with Joshua. Two different planets.

He cooks just for me: a hot peasant soup from Russia, fat stalks of asparagus French style, a bit of veal scallopine, Spanish flan. I feel pleasantly smothered:

What will be you wanting for dinner tonight?

Anything, I am tempted to say, provided it comes with affection.

I hope it will work out for us, says Joshua.

I don't say anything. Do I have hopes? I think I have no emotions left of that sort.

I start two drinks behind,

he says before we go anywhere. His red suspenders hold up his black pants.

When I was little, I would bring home a herring. Ten cents I paid, I would say to my father, who would reprimand me: that's a nine-cent herring.

In the darkness, we set out on the subway, only local service. Two hours later, we arrive at Brighton Beach, and head for the boardwalk. I have a crab all green with spice and some pale yellow white coconut ice. Joshua has a bun stuffed with potato. We walk barefoot on the beach to Coney Island in the cold sand.

What a weekend we will have, says Joshua.

I had a free rental car coming from frequent flyer miles, and he was planning to drive it and me out to Montauk. Waves, gray weather, I pictured it. First, though, he said he was having his last and only cigarette. No problem, he said, I'll just give it up this weekend, don't pay attention to it. When we are away, I will just get over it, and subsist on your affection.

Panic. Sudden memories of my father and the liquor cabinet come rushing in. Dark corridors in the mind. Could he too have subsisted on my affection, had I been more affectionate?

My temples were pulsing.

We had to go to a dinner first. In the grand marble hall of the library, dark suits milling about. Joshua hangs back (shy, he said), his red suspenders now invisible inside his blazer.

No, don't introduce me to anyone, you just go and network,

he said in a low voice, standing by the bar. At the table, his fingers grazed the underside of my wrist. Now suddenly he was no longer there: he must have gone to look for a smoke.

As we left, quarrel was in the air. He needed a cigarette and had none:

You insist, you want things your own way. You want to show me off.

I resisted replying. My tummy was hurting, my head was throbbing, and I longed for my shower. I said I was sorry, whatever I'd done, sniffling. He snapped:

Too much, your tummy and your tears.

I didn't answer, just climbed into the shower to get away from him. After I came out, I was free of tears and of Joshua. He had left in a rage, taking his suitcase away with him, leaving the door to the hall wide open. I went to make myself some tea.

Patrick phoned to chat, and I perched on a high stool in the kitchen to talk with him; it was 12:30 A.M., my favorite time of the day. At 2 A.M, I decided to set off alone in the morning, to Montauk as planned.

Six hours later I was walking toward the 8:20 Hampton Express, with my blue denim knapsack and three apples. Cheaper than the Hampton Jitney, and I was being careful. I settled down in the back with the dissertations I had to catch up with, one on surrealism and my favorite poet, Robert Desnos, almost no corrections to make. Another on Maurice Scève, rather dull, on the relation between the emblems and the text, and how it is mannerist in its style. OK, sure. The third, an intricate theoretical study about futurism, was smart, witty, concise. I was impressed.

I always make my comments in pencil, so the candidates can erase them if they want to, before giving the text to the next reader. This is new for me: younger, I would write always in blue ink. Henri Peyre wrote in purple or brown ink; my poet, René Char, in black ink; André Breton, in green ink.

I got out at Amagansett, browsed around for a while, and caught the next bus for Montauk. Sand, rough water, stones to pick up again, the beach to walk. Chilled, tired, and exhilarated, I returned to my dingy little room.

In the dark, the lights of a small truck over the sand, under the moon. Peter and I, driving along a narrow road on Okrakoke Island, on the Outer Banks of North Carolina, our headlights gleaming on the sand. We are quiet. We don't know where we are heading, or if our long love is ending.

Rain was slanting down on the early ferry to Block Island over the choppy water. The bike rental was closed; I walked the two miles to the few buildings, to the places still open. I should have brought my bike on the ferry, but it all seems magical anyway, rain, exhaustion, all of it.

I settled with a cold beer at Ballard's, at one of the old wooden tables carved up by the years. Joshua just might have phoned, might have missed me, might want to make up. I phone my answering machine. A long message from my novelist friend Frederic Tuten. Where am I, what am I doing, thinking, writing? His warmth spread right through the phone: never close your friends off.

After my steamed clams at three, I walked back to the ferry, still under the downpour, and took the bus home, calm in the darkness. When I returned my apartment, I perched on one of my high stools in the kitchen and phoned Patrick:

I went to Montauk anyway; you are right. When can I see you?

We are close, so alike. We always hold our ears in the subway when a train is coming in, in the movies when there is about to be a gunshot, we look away from scenes of torture. I had to hold my ears even at the sound of the toilet in the plane we took to London: a loud whoosh, unnerving in the small space. Patrick sat on the seat behind me; I would turn around to make sure he was there.

Six

Lectures Here and There

I SPEND A LOT OF TIME traveling about to give lectures on this and that, preparing my slides at home on the lighted tray that stands up on the wooden table. Putting them in some order—a theme emerges sooner or later, and then it all makes sense to me. I find some texts appropriate to the subject, take the books to a place that will make slides for me, and feel, each time, released from the chaos I so often drift into otherwise.

When I look back now, my life seems made up of conferences and meetings of "learned" societies, of these tedious lecture stands, tables draped with cloth, voices droning or impassioned. All these talks, these times, these places, from Melbourne to Manchester, Washington to Winnipeg—I love the travel itself, more than the talks. You have to look interested in all the subjects, I know, so I scribble this or that on a notepad to keep from falling asleep.

BLOOMINGTON, INDIANA

We are all giving lectures on surrealism. My neighbor at the table is J. H. Matthews, a Welshman well known for his vitriolic reviews and attitudes, who once said in public to my then husband, "and how does it feel being her wife? (Pause). Oh, sorry." His pale blue eyes just manage to reach over the handlebar moustache he has grown lately, beneath which is what is, I think, intended to be a faint smile. I read it as very faint indeed. As ironic, in fact. He asks if he can see the text I am about to talk from: it is a jumble of crossed-out lines, which I show him after a slight hesitation. Perhaps that is a twinkle in his eyes as he says, with a sort of grimace, "It makes me sick."

He, of course, reads his lectures from sheets perfectly typed by his wife. Right after his talk, and directly before mine, Jan Kott, the Shakespearean and a former surrealist, rises to protest at the general torpor of the meeting. Quite right, I am thinking, when suddenly the filmmaker Arrabal, to my left at the speaker's table, gets up, removes all his clothes, and streaks down the aisle. I can't remember anything else about that meeting.

INTERNATIONAL FRENCH STUDIES ASSOCIATION, PARIS

I have been invited by a friend—as an honor, I am well aware—to lecture at the Collège de France on visual poetics. Three of the authors I am discussing are right there, facing me. The room has been appropriately darkened for my slides.

I call for the first slide. The image is clearly reversed, as are the next two. It turns out that the person in charge of the projectors is half blind but has been kept on in spite of his advanced age by French politesse. He tries to show me something about the button beneath the podium where you can raise and lower the window shades. *"Ça va, madame?"* he asks. Not so's you'd notice, it doesn't go at all. In fact, it goes from bad to worse: the shades rise when they should fall, and vice versa. I am feeling doomed.

I am the only foreigner lecturing here now, and I have made a mess of things, visually and also verbally. Nothing corresponds to anything intelligible. Laughter, barely suppressed, from the audience. I have embarrassed the friend who invited me, a tall distinguished Australian professor of French, and vastly amused (and also chagrined) my poet friends in the audience: Jacques Dupin, Edmond Jabès, Yves Bonnefoy, and so many others. . . . It is their work, after all, that has been shown backward and upside down.

Mortified, I refuse all the kind offers of being entertained afterward, set off alone in the gathering dark, and regain my room in the Hotel des Grands Balcons (*tiny* balcons, or none, like my room). In the bed, I pull the covers over my head.

ALBANY

I am still rushing about to give lectures: no inclination to stop. I like traveling, like seeing different people, like talking in front of people I don't know:

easier than cocktail parties. There seems to be no reason to stop. I take the train to Albany, along the river, for a lecture on poetry and art sponsored by the New York Humanities Council. I make notes going up: what will I talk about? I have slides, but will have to adjust my words to my pictures:

What kinds of crossover make sense—how foreshortening can work in a painting: Mantegna's body of Christ, say, and ellipsis in a poem. How this kind of not spelling things out can move you. The circularity of some metaphysical poetry, like that of Crashaw, and how it helps you see Georges de La Tour's Mary Magdalene by her candle better. In the Crashaw poem, she weeps tears of repentance to wipe Christ's feet with, and the passion of her hot tears and his blood mounts to the heavens, where the Virgin's milk nourishes the rain, that falls again like tears to the ground, and on it goes. Either you like mannerist and baroque forms of creation or you don't. I do. I love talking about Bernini's Saint Teresa getting religiously stabbed in sculpture, with the spectators watching, and how she hopes the pain will continue, compared to Seghers's painting of Saint Teresa, relating them back to the poems about the saint. The art of interference, as I think of these interactions: maybe I'll do a book on the subject. But I don't have an overarching theory, just perceptions about this and that.

SASKATOON, SASKATCHEWAN

It is the dead of winter, white everywhere. They have put me up in the enormous old railroad hotel, full of luxury and nostalgia. Tonight I'm to lecture on the pre-Raphaelites, how the curtains and cloths all work to frame, but render more mysterious, the personal relations of the figures in the paintings. My slides are ready in their carousels, my laser pointer is in its case, I feel relatively cheerful.

Watch out,

says my host, Len Findlay, himself a well-known authority on this art, tall and tanned, with a gray beard that puts me instantly at ease.

I don't need to say this to someone who travels as much as you, but do be sure not to go walking by yourself outside. Too much snow. No horizon. Would you like to go somewhere with me?

No thanks, I say. I'll be fine. See you later.

I know there's a museum somewhere nearby and prefer looking at paintings alone. Inquiring at the desk, I get instructions and set off, booted, coated, scarved, hatted. No problem.

An hour later, I am lost in the white—you would think I would have known, from all the photographs and films about various expeditions to the Pole, in the snow, that what my host had said was absolutely true. You get lost with no horizon, just in the trackless, featureless white. Little by little, panic overtakes me. No point to anchor the eye on, nothing to break the expanse. At one point I see something that looks like an underground exercise parlor, where people in bright colors are leaping about. Forget the museum, all I know is something has to break the endlessness. I rush into this place with the bodies and the colors and the sounds. And would like to think I had learned some lesson, but probably not.

That evening, I don't mention it to anyone.

OTTAWA

I am to give a talk in Ottawa on a few problems of teaching comparative topics and literature in general, combining the usual processes with art. I want—since it is Canada—to illustrate my talk with Canadian art. In the beating rain and cold, I walk to the National Gallery to see the Veronese and the Poussins, as well as some Canadian art, hoping to pick up some slides. I see the Canadian artists whom I particularly like: Jack Bush, Riopelle, Emily Carr. There are no slides available, but I feel refreshed and energetic, ready. Under the rain, I dash into a taxi to the campus, arriving at the wrong building to give my talk. Not knowing that, I have a bowl of soup for lunch: seafood chowder.

Once I get to the right building, I find the room gratifyingly packed. Excited about showing the two slides I have chosen to begin with in order to speak of conflicting readings, I stride (hoping it looks purposeful) to the back of the room. I put the slides in the projector, and look for my bag with my talk in it: it is nowhere to be seen. I can *show*, but I can't speak. I have arrived before without my slides, but I have rarely arrived like this, speechless. There is always a first time. This is that time. I am crimson.

I seize a book bag from the front table, but it is not mine. Accompanied by someone in the audience, I hasten to the ladies' room, then back to the wrong building in which I lingered and lunched, when I thought it was the right building, finding my bag nowhere. Returning to the room to apologize, miraculously and ridiculously, I find it right there, against the wall, where I had put in the slides. My anxiety must be manifesting itself again.

PARIS

I am presiding over a dullish session at Beaubourg, for a surrealist conference. After every talk, a young frenetic woman, the kind the French call *exaltée,* rises to protest against the Gulf War.

We are all castrated, she says.

No one says anything.

I don't know, she says, if war gives *you* an erection. I am all liquid over it.

No one says anything. I think back to all our protests, wearing armbands at commencement during Vietnam, marching with our children on our shoulders. . . . I smile vaguely. Everyone looks somewhere else.

I think back again. We are in 1974, and this time the conference on surrealism is at the Sorbonne. I am lecturing on Breton's Nadja, *the heartrending story of this man who led a movement honoring, it said and he said, the art of the mad, and who was, as he says, "not up to loving Nadja," because she was exactly that, mad. A beautiful young girl gets up in the back row, and says loudly, "I am Nadja." Everyone looks away.*

This room at Beaubourg is gray, like something masked. I long to leave.

BRYN MAWR COLLEGE

I have been invited to speak at Bryn Mawr. For some reason, I feel shaky about this lecture. I make my way, the walking stick for my twisted ankle going clump clump, heart in my mouth, to the Alumnae House, quiet and set in the snow today.

The sophisticated young lady at the desk, her black hair superbly swept up, smiles at me. I am looking at the picture of my friend Gertrude Ely, an old lady I used to visit, the former owner of this house, famous for importing hockey to the United States, beloved for her eccentric ways.

We used to speak Esperanto together, I say, that lady and I.

She looks at me blankly.

You know, that language made up so everyone could communicate?

Another blank look. She clearly does *not* know. I retreat to my room, clump, clump up the stairs. I must seem very old to her. Maybe I am.

René Girard, my first literature professor, is there for this conference in his honor, on the back row in the center. I have come to honor him. In the middle of my talk, I make a reference to his work on structuralism, walking from the podium to the middle aisle, where I can see him. I gesture to make a point with my cane. The professor is yawning. My professor is yawning, oh god, I must have bored him. We are both embarrassed.

I ask for the lights to be dimmed to show my slides. The main one, a Seurat picture of Chahut, a dance, upon which I have based my entire argument, is too faint to be seen. I try to joke about that, gesturing toward the audience instead of the screen, explaining as I go. When I finish, my respondent replaces my carousel of slides with his own. The first one is the image I was lecturing on, remarkably clear this time.

Ah, I say, did you just focus that better than I did?
No, he replies, this is the painting. You were using the sketch, the one from Buffalo.

And then begins his talk with:

This is the art historian's nightmare: that her technical support will fail.

So it did, but I'm not an art historian, rather a litcrit type. This is meant to be a tease. But I keep thinking why couldn't he have passed me his slide, seeing mine was next to invisible? What would I have done in his place? Is it about turf?

My favorite professor was yawning; my respondent was withholding what I should have been using. But I am less worried than I would have been before. Maybe it doesn't matter as much as I'd thought. Take time to meditate on something here—be aware.

> *I remember years ago, in this very building, which was then the French House, where I used to live, on the top floor. To make some extra money, I showed lantern slides for Dr. Soper, the art history professor. He was very august, and I was very short. The slides were of mixed sorts: color large and small formats, black-and-white large and small formats. I confused them, put some upside down, looked back at Professor Soper, embarrassed. He smiled.*

Hard to get and keep self-confidence. Remember what my father always used to say. It was not a good thing for a lady to work, that he was sure of, from the beginning. Especially one who has been fortunate enough to grow up in the South. He was never to change his mind, especially about his younger daughter. If I was absolutely determined to do something, I most certainly (being a young lady) should not be *paid* for it. He would remind me of this from time to time, when I was trying to secure a teaching post.

> But don't you think I should support myself?
> I trust, my dear, you will never have to.

That was about where the conversation would stop. There wasn't much room for it to go anywhere else.

When I had a contract with Princeton for my first real book after the tiny one that Mouton in Holland had published from my dissertation, I telephoned home at once, positive that this time, I would have done something Father could approve of. There was a long silence. Followed by a question, asked in a low voice, by Mother, to whom Father must have communicated the news.

> Will you be writing them a thank-you letter, dear?

I was stunned into silence.

> Because if so, *do* thank them for us too, for your father and myself. They are really too kind.

The self-confidence I had been trying to build up made a rapid exit: I should have been prepared for this, and was not.

BALTIMORE, MARYLAND

I am giving the keynote speech, in Baltimore, for the southern branch of the Modern Language Association, on the relation between text and image. There are a fair number of listeners. But the microphone suddenly seems too grand for my talk, and I have to move about to discuss the slides I have brought. I discard the mike, without asking if I can be heard. (No, I couldn't, but no one said anything.) Later, it occurs to me this is childish behavior. My intuition of the moment overrrules my better judgment: it is all of a piece.

LONDON, BBC STUDIOS

Here to lecture on surrealism, for the Tate Modern show. After a long hesitation about coming over, after 9/11 and all that, I have arrived, still feeling shaky. The pilot on our plane came out and warned us not to go into the aisles, not to cause any commotion: I am a New Yorker, he said, don't mess with me.

Me, I think, I'm a newer New Yorker, but how could I ever say that?

Many of us gathered on the stage, one speaker from each field. One on psychoanalysis and surrealism, one musician, one this, one that. An interviewer from the BBC, and the actor Simon Russell Beale reading my translations of surrealist poets: Robert Desnos, Paul Eluard, André Breton, Benjamin Péret, Joyce Mansour. . . . I suspected the question would arise and that I wouldn't know how to handle it:

> People say the attack on the Twin Towers was surrealist. What do you think of that use of the term?

I cannot remember what I said. It changed everything. But how do you talk about what's changed, in a city or in your mind? Forget surrealist: I hate the adjective anyway. It is a noun for me.

MADISON, WISCONSIN

Here I am, to lecture on modernism and the visual arts. Obviously, the topic is far too large, and I cut it down to a few moments in the twentieth century that seem of most importance to me: cubism, futurism, Dada, surrealism, constructivism. Last week, in Florida, I was talking on the same topic but choosing different pieces to mark the moments—prevents boredom, if you have to react to different images and forms. There, in the heat, I splashed about in the pool—what luxury for an adopted Manhattanite!—took a glass of wine outside to a table and tried to concentrate on what I thought modernism was.

Like all those times in the Rose Cafe in Venice, when I was a Getty Scholar, and would bike there to sit outside, under the jacaranda tree with its orange blossoms and a glass of wine or some coffee and a long, long cinnamon twist, trying to think, write, be. I was better at being when I was outside. Better at thinking too.

California, Florida, why wouldn't I live there . . . because I can't drive any distance without falling asleep at the wheel. Because of my friends. That is enough to keep me in New York, having my coffee in the boathouse in Central Park. Or by the sailboat lake.

That's where I do my thinking and daydreaming.

Above all I long to get to the Louise Bourgeois exhibition on State Street, past all those stores with bright clothing and games, past the outside market, reminding me of the Second Street market in Santa Monica, that Getty year . . . apples, cheeses, wooden toys . . . toward the City Center. The minute I am surrounded by art I care about, I feel myself once more. You can walk between those person-high sculptures of her Woman Carrying . . . and some Child or other. The smooth wooden forms, the simplified structures. Here you can lose yourself and find yourself. I go up the stairs to the video— fourteen minutes, it says—of her being interviewed in her studio, strong faced, impressive, a model for us all.

Then I rush back, late for my session. Why am I always rushing? The moderator has already announced the titles and the participants, and my seat at the table is noticeably empty, in the middle of the three men already seated. Ah, the moderator is saying, I don't know if she will get here.

No, no, she will, I mean she did, she is me,

I say, to guffaws all around me. Later, giving the paper, it is as if I had to make room for myself all over again, until I settle back into the topic.

GUGGENHEIM MUSEUM

Here to lecture on Dada, to prepare the audience for a brief opera by a Czech Dadaist called Martinu. I dress in black, with a red scarf, to look the Dada part. And concentrate on one of my favorite works, Marcel Duchamp's *Tu m'*, from the Yale Art Gallery. I've written and spoken about this work before, how it is about the traces of some of his ready-mades and experiments—the *Stoppages-Etalons*, the coatrack, the bicycle wheel, like one of his portable valises or boxes with his works in miniature form.
How works can be contained—I think of Henry James's *Golden Bowl*, and how it contains the idea of itself . . . keep your mind from wandering.

So how do I speak of the title? About its incompletion, not hard to speak: it is short for *Tu m'emmerdes*, so, it really means Fuck Off, how to say that without scandalizing the people who invited me. I say: well, it means, um, you bore me, bother me, or um, something stronger. Yes, nod some heads in the audience, we know. Now I feel really stupid. Tomorrow night, I say to myself, when I have again to give this demonstration—more like that than a lecture, in fact—I will say it outright.

I do, and who cares? Must be some southern hangup about propriety that trips me up.

TEACHING IN NEW YORK

Lecturing in my own classes was different. I ended up loving whatever I taught, particularly when I could include art with the texts. I'd talk about how a diagonal reading can be used, specifically in a poem, to make more interesting parallels between syntax and imagery than the ordinary linear

left-to-right pattern the Western eye is used to following. I'd demonstrate in
a painting how such diagonals are stressed, either in straight lines or in ser-
pentine ones—as in the mannerist weavings back and forth of Tintoretto's
Leda and the Swan, for example, comparing it then with Yeats's poem by the
same name. Then I'd compare it with some other Ledas and some other
swans of literature and art, and then perhaps extend the branchings into
other kinds of swans, black and white: of Baudelaire and Mallarmé, of
Ruben Darío and Neruda and Thomas Mann, before the curve of that neck
reaches back into art, and Leda has her time to develop. These classes I loved.

But of course there are always other things: committees, dissertations, and
exams, the latter of which I rarely enjoyed. One day, we were sitting, three
colleagues, myself, and a Ph.D. student being examined on her knowledge
of literature and philosophy, around a table in a seminar room whose only
window opens onto a yellow brick wall. This room was generally dedicated
to philosophy seminars. On the blackboard was written, in a careful hand,
to the right of a series of diagrams:

Be Sure, at All Times, to State Your Premise Clearly!
and under it was scrawled:

so this is logic?

Something about that setup struck me as very funny: the relatively successful
put-down and the unwitting solemnity of the command. I tried to bring my
attention back to the matter at hand, examining his student whom I consid-
ered not very bright. She was a budding comparatist who wished to write a
thesis entitled something like "Certain Philosophies and the Work of Samuel
Beckett." The part I was supposed to examine her on was not philosophy
but Beckett, about whom she had so far seemed, alas, to know relatively
little.

Some critic, she had said in her written proposal, had pointed out the link
with Schopenhauer and I was eager or at least willing to hear that discussed.
She had not provided us with the name of the critic, nor with any suggestion
of the link proposed. I asked for details, giving what I judged to be my most
reassuring smile: the kind that reveals how you are interested, patient, sure
that we are on our way to a fascinating discussion.

I have a problem, said the young woman, twisting a button on her
blouse, with Schopenhauer.

Ah, I said, retaining my most patient smile, and wondering in that case why she would have brought up the comparison.
You have a problem with Schopenhauer. Now we are on to something, surely. What is it exactly? Do you think Beckett might have had the same problem?

Silence. "Perhaps your problem is with Beckett," I longed to say, but bit my tongue. No point.

Well, would you like to talk of some other philosophers and Beckett? Any other philosopher, I added, looking at her vacant expression.
Take anyone. I paused, and continued hoping now that I was in my patient mode. Take any relation between Beckett and someone.

Silence. I am plainly not able to summon forth answers in this case. What exactly was the problem, and whose? It was getting to be mine.

OK. Take Joyce and a philosopher, and show how the relation might differ between that combination and, say, Beckett and some thinker. Anyone.
So can I talk about Leibniz? I don't have a problem with Leibniz.
Sure, go on.

I look at my colleagues, Michael with his lavender T-shirt bringing out the blue of his eyes behind his horn-rimmed glasses; Angus with his long-ish light gray hair and sparkling eyes—even his nose is witty. Two thousand other people and I have always admired Angus. The third member of our company I knew less well. That's probably a good thing; I had heard him often state his conviction that women have inferior brains, a statement he seemed to make without irony. I found myself wishing the candidate were male, not wanting him to have ammunition for his persuasion. Damn.
He smiled a bit at my question, tossing his head back until its blond waves rested on his green corduroy jacket where it met the chair. His neck was crimson. It was always that color.

My dear Mary Ann, he uttered the name like some sort of medicine. Let me see if I can rephrase your most challenging questions. Might we not rather see it this way? The point was, and even is, if I am not sorely mistaken, to invite Ms. Peders—Jane (here came his smarmy smile)—to discuss certain philosophers and not certain relations, if you see what I mean.

My face felt as crimson as his neck. But of course I saw what he meant all right.

Ms. Peders was looking relieved: let's get away from this crazy woman and her snide questions and back on the pleasing-the-man track, shall we? I looked around the table, and decided just to do the general kind of question and call it quits.

Right, Ms. Peders, so sorry; why don't you just tell us what you find most interesting about this topic?
Oh, you know. It is important for the modern psyche.

I waited. That couldn't be it, that could not possibly be the end of what she was going to say? I had to help her save some sort of face.

How?

She picked up the question; her face suddenly lit up:

Maybe we can even say, for modernism. I believe that is true for Derrida and everybody. Lacan, Kristeva, you know, everybody.

I kneaded my hands together under the table. Mustn't snort: be polite, attentive, kind. Think of a question she can grip. My mind went blank.

Could you elaborate, please? asked Michael.

I was grateful to him for asking. Every time I asked anything, the ground sort of scooted away under my feet.

Oh, you devil! She simpered at him.

I loathed all this, and had wanted just to make a point: how to do it? That: you can't just flirt, wink, and simper your way through what is supposed to be a serious trial of the intellect and the imagination. On the other hand, I was beginning to feel like a prude. Is this what my energy has turned into, a condemnation of the erotic interplay of others? Heavens.

Ms. Peders, I started over. Perhaps . . . Look, let's talk about Beckett. What is your basic approach to whichever text you feel most comfortable with? Which genre do you find yourself attracted to?

I hate myself for this dummy question, loaded with traps. Give her enough rope, I was thinking. Then, to my utter surprise, Ms. Peders turned out to be more knowledgeable than I could have guessed, once she settled down to a text. She had chosen Watt, my all-time favorite, and was actually saying things I'd never thought of.

My mind went back to long ago, when I was in exactly her position. At Yale, feeling out of sorts, sure no one understood my projects, my way of thinking, when suddenly I was given the occasion to choose, to talk about the poet I found most compelling; the world opened up. The faces around me, I'll never forget the moment, seemed to change their dull, cynical, and uncomprehending blankness to vital witnesses of thinking beings. I never understood the alteration or tried to: the key was in my choice and not my perception.

What was happening here, in my own place, with my own colleagues, with myself, was what had happened to me all those years before. I had continued because of that moment.

What could I say? Afterward, I took Ms. Peders aside and smiled at her hesitant face: it was up to me now.

I'm so sorry. You just proved you have it in you; I couldn't see it. What about a cup of coffee?

Summer School, Dartmouth

All summer, teaching in the Theory School at Dartmouth: I'd been invited to give a seminar on the relation between literature and the visual arts.

I wake up at 3:46 A.M., for my usual middle-of-the-night read, this time with a specific memory, of skipping down a hill too fast, and the world going blurry, somehow joined with a memory of being with Peter in Edinburgh on a misty day when there was dew on the grass behind the museum. We'd seen a small painting of bright flowers with dew on them, and we'd been happy. We'd gone out holding hands, in our raincoats, Peter with his gaunt face, heavy brows, and kind eyes. I'd seen a slope that looked just right, on the hill in the center of town, and was afraid to embarrass him by trying it. He grinned, reached out to take my coat, and down I went, ungainly I expect, but delighted to feel the coarseness of the grass prickling under my blouse as I rolled, just the way I had so many times behind the Washington Cathedral. And like the somersaults you could do in the large pool here, with its lanes marked with bright ribbons. I would come up sideways. What did I have to roll about, somersault about, again all at once?

Describe the day. We had gone early, Noel Perrin the writer and I, Ned with those deep creases in his cheeks under his white shock of hair and his black glasses, to a general store, on the way to his farm in Thetford. We had looked at watering cans (green plastic, orange plastic, off-white plastic, but none of plain tin, as he had hoped), and then that off-white crockery with blue stripes you found in Carrier's in London but also in Dayton, Ohio, and finally, some grab hooks. We talked about cheeses and pumpernickel bread, and how we liked our rye in irregular slices. The floor seemed sort of high to me when he was around, and it would bounce a little under our feet.

We would sit at the wooden table in the kitchen of his farmhouse, looking out over those hills with the fern high by the window . . . there is just one channel on my TV here, he said, and that is it. We had the bread and cheese and some tomatoes (to-mah-toes, he said), tasting like Provence, over the leaves of two different lettuces he grew.

I asked Ned my question about who knelt to whom at Canossa, so we looked it up, in the eleventh edition of the Britannica, where he claimed he got the better part of his knowledge. Then we lay on the grass outside his farmhouse, biting into our watermelon slices, and throwing the rind into the shrubbery. He taught me how to call his sheep (cree-ah), and they stuck their heads through the wire. The wool was stiffer than I would have thought. Then we called the cows (sum-pah), and they lumbered along toward us. I went to get more grain and took it across the road to them. Like a child, I thought, but so happy. We walked along stepping on the cowpats not yet hard, and later, toward the covered bridge, red against the lurid green of the meadow.

We walked then past the roses, striped and regular, and he picked the smallest for taking home, and afterward on a path by the river. If we'd had a dog, it would have come too, and lain down contented on the mossy rock, above the water where we saw the trees reflected upside down. Then, at twi-light, we swam in the river, Ned in his faded green trunks. He stood on an overlying rock, talking to a neighbor, before jumping in gently so as not to splash me. We slithered down over the shallow parts to where we could pile up some stones, sitting in the water. He always built, I thought to myself, little dams and stone walls. Something so haunting about him and his mind.

We walked down the waterfall, slipping a little on the stones with moss on them, and lay down again to look at the light. Dappled light, I said, and he:

I'm always ready to talk about dappled light,

and then we swerved to silence. I didn't know if he was sleeping, in that glancing light. Dappled, really. And later we walked back by the covered bridge.

Other days, we'd pick raspberries, just a few, for they were not yet ripe, leaving a few quarters by the stand not yet open. A few days later, we re-turned to pick a half pint each, leaving our little boxes a bit empty: "like the Japanese," he said. And we gathered blackberries for the neighbor's child, her mouth smeared with jam. Often Ned would lie on the grass or the floor, as if exhausted. And always, we would look, before I went home, at how the fieldstone was gray, heavy and yet somehow light. Everything that summer had to be light: all that swimming in those foam-flecked rivers, all that time we spent speaking of so much, by those waterfalls with reddish banks, all those days of calling sheep and cows and looking at walls he made and mended.

Because I wouldn't be staying here either. Traveling light: I was always leaving.

Seven

New York Journal

December 1992

I'VE BECOME VERY MUCH attached to a doctor Pat introduced me to last year; Boyce plays the piano, knows about music, and has a face I think of as noble. I worry—of course I worry—it won't last. It's as if I never felt anyone could be attached to me over a long period. All the same, I've rarely been so happy. The way people smile at us in the street when we walk by. The way he leans his shoulder against mine. The particular clarity of his face sometimes.

I worry my excitement over this will exhaust him. The days we spend seem to me the most delightful I've ever known; the park bench we sit on holding hands seems the nicest bench ever; the dogs cavorting down the hill the most elegant imaginable; the air so crisp it tingles. I try not to say much. My enthusiasm wears people out. Peter to begin with, and I don't want this to end as that did.

But such perfect days. Last Saturday we had a pastrami sandwich at Wolf's delicatessen, and a cognac at the Saint Moritz, watched a tennis match on TV, went to three art galleries, had an espresso by the bamboo trees in the IBM building, and took home some clams. Then he picked up his Bach invention again, on his blond piano, now repainted black: the invention his mother was playing once—the time he told me about—the tears streaming down her face. Late in the evening, we sipped some brandy and had a few blueberries, their taste exploding in our mouths.

You make me so happy,

I say, touching the crease in his cheek.

You make me happy too. Have another blueberry.

How long would this last, I wonder, hoping I won't ever ask it aloud.

One day, we were walking in the sun along the Hudson at Wave Hill, and stopped for lunch, overlooking the river.

You choose a sandwich for us, he said.

After picking up a dried tomato and mozzarella on a baguette, with two glasses of raspberry iced tea, I took the platter outside, where he'd chosen a wooden bench, and was looking at the water and the Palisades beyond.

What would you want to make this perfect?

he asks. Nothing, I think. Come up with something, I must, to keep the same tone.

Oh, I don't know, not that bedraggled palm.

You know what I would want—mountains with snow on top.

I knew that and much else, some of it indefinite and fearsome, some clear. He was never going to want what I want, of course that was bound to be it. Like Peter. Like everyone. I must be giving off beams of loneliness.

That day, we didn't say much, just looked at the flowers in the garden, at the peonies that always seemed too large. At the begonias, the roses, the delphinium, the dianthus, and other flowers I can't remember. We seldom looked at each other. Though I'd have liked us to. In the greenhouse, the light poured down on the impatiens plants he was getting for his apartment. White and pink.

Another day it was ninety-one degrees outside, and the parade up Third Avenue had large floats saying Jesus Loves You. He was playing his piano in shorts. Brahms, I think, and the chords were very loud. I wonder the Tiffany lamp, blue green, intricate, sitting atop the piano didn't tremble. When I sat by his side on the bench, waiting to turn the page, sometimes I would look at the fingering in pencil on the score, and sometimes at the lamp. I tried not to look at the crease in his cheek.

When the dusk fell, he turned on the lamp, lovingly, I thought.

But one day I said to myself that this would never work out. Look at my past, look at my family's past. . . . I should have known. Numb, I placed on the front table the few pieces he had lent me: four records, two books. I was not prepared for his reaction.

Ah, I see you have put out all my things.

His face had a funny look. I didn't know what to make of it, now that I was almost certain there was nothing to be made of us. Or so it seemed to me. Like always. Of course you shouldn't trust people to stick to you. That heavy weight in my heart again. How could it feel like a hole and a heavy weight at once?

Of course I'd gotten his things out for him. That's what you do, isn't it? you give back what is lent you, and you smile. No resentment. All grown-ups here.

> *My mind goes back to years ago: I am taking out all Peter's clothes from the closet in our bedroom where he has left them, putting them in a great burlap postal bag and setting it in the front room where he can pick it up. The pattern on the rug has diamonds in it. I used to stare at it when he was first with his girlfriend, and Hilary the baby would frolic on it in her Babygro, while the sunlight picked out the reds in particular. Now I am phoning my husband's answering machine to say: "they are there, your clothes, and I am not." My voice is wavering badly. Dammit. I had so wished I could rerecord it, smile on the phone.*

What I miss the most is belonging. To whom do I belong? And now, what had I put out now? Just those records and the books.

The books are for you. Don't you want to listen to the records anymore?

No, I thought, too much pain. But I couldn't talk about that, it would burden him.

OK, I said. Thanks. I will.

I remember when Matthew moved out of the studio Peter and I used to write in. We had to remove the furniture, strip the place, undo the bookcases—it felt like undoing the self. So did this.

Now his face swims in front of the page I read, the lines I write, the meals I cook for myself. He used to phone every night. I pick up the phone several times an hour to be sure it is working. I often practice sounding light and funny so—if he did call—it wouldn't weigh on him. I kept trying so hard not to be needy, because I know that's what weighs on people.

I looked at myself in the mirror to be sure that the next time we met I could do the wry smile, the well-I'm-pretty-happy one, and how are *you?* Accent on the *you.* It's supposed to sound like this:

Me, I'm *fine* (high-low, sounds more convincing). How are *you?* (different high-low, takes practice).

What happened to honest straightforwardness, the kind that used to be so precious? When I could say, without even hesitating:

Look, I'd really like to *see* you. When can we get together?

I couldn't get his voice out of my mind. The way it used to say:

Call me when you get home,

with the tone rising to "get" and then rounding off lower, at the "home," on two descending notes. Why do we always have the same tones to say the same things?

It isn't just a gesture I miss, or a voice, but a whole way of shaping an evening, a life. I would come in, go to the answering machine, hearing just those tones I expected. It wasn't so much the calling or being asked to call as the habit of it.

Like the way you know if you look up in the evening, at the top of those buildings on, say, Forty-seventh and Madison, there will be a little mass of clouds curling gray or sometimes pink around them. The way, in the morning, the mist will be hanging over the boat pond in Central Park. The two large dogs will be sniffing around to see what they can pick up, their masters conversing loudly about books, rare and less so, at one of the white tables. These things I can count on, echoing down the years. But not that voice.

Oh, he calls every two or three days now, at irregular times, in varying moods. He can't be counted on, any more than I can. What can? Well, says

Patrick, you are bound to meet someone better for you, you know, who will understand. This is just a quirky year for you: it will pass. Let the whole idea go. Do what Zen counsels: when the thought of something comes, surround it with a balloon and send it off.

So many more important things, I know, I know. People are blowing each other up; Salman Rushdie's publishers are having to unlist their phone numbers; people are dying of starvation and loneliness everywhere; and I am full of too-muchness. How to disengage from excess? Too much emotion, too much pain, too much self-absorption.

Now in Central Park, the snow covers the ground. There's the tree we used to sit under, to read and just look around. Sometimes leaning on the trunk, sometimes on each other. We never talked much. Maybe we'd read aloud to each other a sentence or so and then plunge back in our own pages.

Just the memory remains. As if it were all about nostalgia, longing backward. When you know you have to move on. Letting the past go, the snow cover the ground you sat on, turning the pages blindly. Letting go.

The phone rings.

You're there, he says. Want to take a walk?

We walk past the same place, with the same memories. He stops a moment:

Remember that tree? Didn't we sit there last summer?

I don't say anything, not trusting my voice. What we don't have to say is that something may have been covered under the snow. It shouldn't matter. He smiles at me, and we resume our walk, not looking back at the tree.

We go back to his apartment. On the piano the Tiffany lamp sits, blue with a green tinge, the top spreading out like an umbrella with a delicate round sweep.

Trust is such a risk.

January 2, 1993

I can't get Peter's voice out of my mind either. We would sit by the East River and watch the tugboats. His grandfather piloted one, he would say, and look off in the distance. We would sit very still. I am sitting very still now, learning how to do that. Dash around less.

· First thing in the morning, after you say what you're grateful for, say what you don't want to lose.

> Trust what you know, says Gerhard.
> You can do it, Mummy, says Hilary.
> We are here for you, says Matthew.

Be there for them, I say to myself, that's what matters. Then I'll be there for myself.

March 22, 1993

Anything at Columbia still makes me nervous, I never figured out why. Tonight I came in late to a theory of literature seminar, and plunked myself down at one end of a long table upstairs in the Faculty Club. I couldn't see who was at the other end, on my side, but was suddenly taken with a panic. It had a beard, a balding pate, and was leaning forward. Was it Joshua? It might have been: the talk is in his area tonight, and he's a local. My heart was pounding, I could feel my feverish face, and trembling hands trying to steady themselves on the hard surface. I tried to take some notes, but the lines went wiggly. The wallpaper was checked, and worn off in spots. I couldn't leave, in this small number of people. Why did I come?

No, it was not anyone I knew. I was bored, no longer nervous, but bored. Maybe we don't have to do things that don't interest us, just because we think we should. Try to do without the concept "should," says Baylis.

April 28, 1993

The boathouse looks the same as always. Bikes, dogs, children running around. Bird-watchers. By the boat lake, some of the red and green weathered rowboats have survived, but they are being replaced by newer ones, less character I think. Now even a gondola.

Twenty years is a long time to keep going somewhere, and it feels like home to me. I listen to the chairs scraping across the floor and they sound just the way they used to. If something happened to the boathouse, where would they all go? those photographers, the gravel-voiced man, the taxi drivers in their checked shirts, and the unsmiling lady with her thick accent, frowning at her portable radio always on the classical station? where would any of us go?

I am teaching *To the Lighthouse*. In my more idealistic moments, I think of gathering all my friends around, like Mrs. Ramsay doing her boeuf en daube, knitting people together by candlelight, at some table, with the lighthouse beams coming in, or whatever the New York equivalent might be. I love its having been Roger Fry's recipe. . . .

These balmy evenings, you'd like to be biking somewhere, for a supper by a lake, maybe. With a fish frying peacefully over some fire. Or a walk by the ocean. Even on the New York streets, a smell of somebody's barbecue in the air.

September 22, 1993

I have decided to go down to the Barnes Collection, just to remember how it was when I went there from Bryn Mawr. It is like old times. I take the Paoli local from the train station in Philadelphia to Merion. My heart is pounding.

All the pictures I remembered were there, the Cézannes and Matisses and Picassos crowding each other, on top of each other, every one calling for attention. Today they seem to be full of moral lessons, about sharpness, slope, certainty, clarity:

The way the young girl with a red vest in the Cézanne picture is looking out to my left. Her ears are protruding, her hair is parted in the middle, and she is slouching in her chair. The older lady in the preposterous hat, like a platter with heaped-up ivy in the center, is looking out to my right, sitting sideways in her chair, her hands clasped, she is all blues and greens against the brown curve of the chair. Above her, a tiny still life by Renoir, a blue china cup, four oranges, and two bananas. The flesh tones enter the fruit and round it out. A funny correspondence between the hat and the fruit above it.

There are four peaches in this still life. The slope of the plate, white with blue. I think: how can I get a better *slant* on things. Beneath it, a gardener, sightless, mouthless, sheathed in bright green, leaning on his spade. The warm orange colors of the ground set my eyes stinging. The intensity of the branch of the tree. Cézanne painting until his eyes were red. Rilke's letters to Clara, his wife, about Cézanne.

Another Cézanne, just of a branch sweeping across gray trees, with a wide central space. Like the angle of a broad snowplow when you are cross-country skiing. Sometimes, the dapple of his trees, orange and green. More dappled things.

The rich chocolate brown of copper in a Chardin. A wine vat and copper basin against the iron and the black of a jug. The gleam of the whole scene. Keep the slant and the gleam. When the cabbage is green and the top of the copper pot is slightly off, the copper gleams differently, like the carrot alongside.

A tiny Seurat, with four sailboats and a high horizon. Matisse, Braque: a lemon, a spoon, a glass of water by a white plate. It is enough. Another Matisse, its yellow frame protruding into the room: sharp, certain. Clear shapes: I think my outlines are sometimes muddy.

Clarity of outline: I love Mark Doty's description in *Still Life with Oysters and Lemon,* named after a painting by Jan Davidsz de Heem from more than 350 years ago that he saw at the Met. It was exhibited in a glass case "so that one bends and looks down into its bronzy, autumnal atmosphere. . . . It *is* an atmosphere; the light lovingly delineating these things is warm, a little fogged, encompassing, tender, ambient. As if, added to the fragrance evoked by the sharp pulp of the lemon, and the acidic wine, and the salty marsh-scent of the oysters were some fragrance the light itself carried." And afterward: "We are all walking in the light of a wedge of lemon, four oysters, a half-glass of wine, a cluster of green grapes with a few curling leaves still attached to their stem." I have walked in the light of so many paintings. . . .

The thick brightness of Van Gogh's roofs: red, green, yellow. You don't need sadness in things.

In a Giorgione, two men are looking down. I think of a poetry that would look away.

All the visitors today are wearing purples and mauves and gray: There is a great calm. I am dressed in white, black, and gray. I fit here. I am most at home in museums and department stores, places of anonymity, where you're just what you're looking at.

Then with all that crowding in my mind, I took the Paoli Local back to Philadelphia. An uplifting notice for children, in bright colors, is right in front of me:

You Believe What Your Parents Tell You

Yes, I think, I guess you do. I hope I have told my children the right things. If not, there's time to do so still. And to tell myself.

I rush onto the Metroliner to New York, eager to get back. We arrive in New York. Outside the station I bless the sidewalks in New York, how back home it feels. My source of energy. On the grubby beloved building to my right, I read what feels like Old New York poetry, in a classic vein:

> BO-PEEP undies
> HIGH STYLE
> gowns
> pajamas
> Sam Landorf Co.
> Creators of clothes for infants
> and children
> Also Better Blouses
> PLAYTOGS

I hear myself saying aloud, to no one in particular, about us all, I guess: "We live here." I'm getting my mind back again.

October 3, 1993

Every time I enter the park on my bike from East Seventy-ninth Street in the fall, it is like entering a whole field of orange color. Two dogs scamper down the hill, and I think how I love the word scamper, as well as the sight of it. *Scampering.*

Today the trees seem heavier than usual, and you can look down to the lake through them. I walk to the right, where the coffee is, and find one of the white tables unoccupied. The others have groups of dog lovers and dogs, the people all talking and the dogs all barking. I love it: this is my New York. The way the long branch is parallel to the green water. The way the fall wasp hovers over my cup, seeming not to know it's the wrong season.

The man sweeping up the leaves, while the immense long-haired sheep-dog sits on the wall watching him. Patrick's voice on the phone last night: how we talk for hours about anything. I went to weed the other day in his rose garden near the cathedral: his careful labeling of them—Bianca, Chaucer, the Dark Lady, Bel Ami. Blue spikes and daisies.

He has sent Peg some roses for her garden: they are very close.

Make a wide network, says Patrick. That way you won't get so lonely.

It was with Patrick that I first heard myself laugh again. At the Cathedral of Saint John the Divine, I remember: we were watching Philippe Petit climb up a rope above the main altar, in step with a Bach aria. It was no time to laugh, but I was happy.

Look now, I used to say to Patrick, when we would spend our week-ends together. We might be sitting in the Peacock Cafe, having our favorite caffe latte. Look how the waiter is smiling, I would say. Look at us. Look how we settle down at any little table we see, look how we are used to each other.

Sometimes I write Peg.

Why are you so far away? I tease her.

She knows it means: Isn't it great we are so close it doesn't matter where we are.

Then I phone Patrick to lament about feeling out of sorts. My ankle hurts, I am lonely, I don't know how to finish all the things I've promised to write.

Don't worry, he says brightly; we won't last long.

April 12, 1994

I am tired of wandering, tired of visiting here, teaching there, trying things out everywhere. I have come back.

Of course, once in New York again, teaching again at the Graduate School of the City University, I feel besieged by duties. But that is what it is about, isn't it?

Carl, one of my dissertation students, phoned early, before I left for the boathouse on my bike.

Ah, how lucky I am. You're *there*.
Of course I am,

I say to him and myself, of course, where else should I be? and I can be counted on. That's it, I want to be countable on, to be stable, to be here.

> Count on me, I practice saying to myself. I say it to the mirror, trying to look convincing. *Count* on me.
> Meet me at the boathouse, I say to Carl. You know, you walk over from Fifth. Bring your last chapter, we'll take a look.

This is the room of my own I have chosen. This is the place where my mind can see what is around it. The place the seasons change from, in front of. The lake, iced over. The lake, with boats on it in summer and spring. Where a seagull can soar, or dip. For thirty years, I've watched this lake, living.

This is where I live in my mind.

Today, on my way from the sailboat lake up to the James Michael Levin Playground, a social worker was interviewing a worker in his overalls. Earnest, with her yellow notepad:

> Maybe you can relate by telling me your feelings.

He did not answer, his fork was digging in his lunch.

A snowman was melting in the sun with his earth showing through. A father held up his little son to whirl him around:

> See the snowman? See the snowballs? Look!

Later that night Matthew and I were perched at the bar of Hurricane Island, waiting for Hilary. He had bought me some calcium tablets, and I had bought him a drink. He had a few great musical admirations these days, including Leonard Cohen, Dylan, and, still, Billie Holliday. Me, it's still Glenn Gould.

> Can people change? I asked him.
> They can, says Matthew. I have.

March 21, 1995

How things vanish when you don't write them down. The tiniest things: the good places to lean over to tie your shoelaces on the old sneakers that are constantly untying themselves. The way some people smile at you in the street when you walk by.

On Park Avenue, in the center of the traffic lanes, some green shoots are pushing up through the snow. My fingers are freezing on my bike handles, but I stop to take from a pole the blank part of an announcement about someone willing to move for you, someone willing to paint for you. I don't have anything to paint or to move, but I love simply to scribble on the paper, in that exaltation of the early morning, that excitement of having too much to do.

With my colleague Gerhard, I've been having brunch every Saturday for as long as I can remember. Just like Patrick, there's nothing we can't talk about. He listens to everything with concentration.

> Cement yourself into reality, Gerhard says. And calm down, there's always time. You don't have to scribble, you can just type it out neatly.

No, I cannot. It will be gone. Joseph Cornell trying to hold on to his experiences, scribbling on napkins to mark his place in books, on catalogues, on envelopes, on record jackets, on anything he could find, cluttering up his study, his diary, his life, but caring so much to get everything down. Not to forget ever any moment.

I'm on my way home, early, to the boathouse, on my bike. Once in the park, I feel free. There's something about the wonderful aloneness you have on a bicycle, right out in the world and yet away. I remember Peg's telling me about some of her favorite moments, two about bikes. One day she wasn't at school—some glorious small sickness—but out on her bike alone on the uneven sidewalk, with the pines rustling overhead and the sand under her tires a newly washed white; another, when she was older, on her bike in Cape Cod, with the wind blowing up just before a storm and the clouds scudding by in the gray sky overhead.

My home is in the middle of Central Park. Like an anchor, that dilapidated building welcomes me. I am nervous until I finally push open the green door and go past the telephone—where I sometimes call Carolyn to see if we can walk, or Matthew, to see if he can join me. At the counter, a few desultory remarks, the hot cup between my cold fingers.

I choose a table inside, by the windows, leave it for the terrace, where the old men are still sunning themselves with reflecting foil collars under their chins. I put my feet in their white Reeboks up on the railing, see the snow beneath the terrace, the ducks swimming in the lake delighted between the banks, the trees losing their white profiles as the sun starts up.

April 20, 1995

This morning I found in the hall a Chinese fortune, one of those small slips we believe and don't believe in.

Learn how to live; you won't have a second chance.

I walked up the street, had a coffee and read the paper, feeling like me again. I lingered. No need to rush around any more. Then I went into a plant shop and stood there for a few minutes, just surrounded by the green. Things seemed calm here, voices lower. I asked for some instructions about growing herbs on my windowsill, then went to the bike store for a new pump. When I was given a choice of colors, I took bright blue, the color of those cornflowers I had at my marriage long ago. I carried the pump home, pumped up my bike tires, and rode off through the park, feeling like springtime.

December 2003

This afternoon, Matthew and I had a peanut butter milkshake in EJ's Luncheonette where you get the metal container with the frost on it. Last week Boyce went with me to hear him play at the Knitting Factory—we put in our foam earplugs purchased for the occasion and laughed—the volume was right, and we were together. Thunderous applause, you could hear it right through the earplugs. Hilary would have loved it—maybe we'll go hear him play the next time she comes down. She's writing away in her little house, beautiful as ever. Her essays have an upbeat turn, like some of Matthew's music, and she runs marathons.

I've just seen my face in the mirror. Always a surprise. I look like my father, a thing I used to regret; but he had spunk and moral strength. My chin sticks out like his, as if I were determined. Don't know to do what.

Last night I dreamt of Mother in a flowered dress, although she never wore a flowered dress to my knowledge. She was dancing, rather a modern dance, strangely not her style. She smiled at me and went on dancing. I would have told Carolyn, but she's not here anymore.

April 2004

Now that I look at it, my journal seems always to have been about coming home . . . no matter where I was. Or trying to find a home to come home to. In my apartment there is a small bench we used to have at home in North Carolina; it holds a chaotic pile of books. The smooth plaster torso of the Unknown Woman my grandmother had always by her side sits on an old carved metal chest she brought back from Bremen, where she lived until the First World War. On my favorite kitchen shelf there is the tiny cup from Brittany, of Quimper pottery, that she had in Paris: it is not marked with a number, as some of the more recent vintage pieces are—it is as old as she would be now. On the longest wall of my apartment, there hangs the tapestry we had in our front hall, with a dog who looks at you wherever you turn.

Nothing else of our old house remains here, where I have lived so differently from the way we used to, Peg and I, so far from the parents we lived with. Hilary works with computers for library programs, has adopted part of a road, and helps in an animal shelter. She and Jonathan are putting on plays in upstate Pennsylvania. Matthew's rock/pop group, Nada Surf, is a great success, in Europe as in the U.S., and he is happy. As for me, I am still taking the risk of trust.

Eight

Returns

HILARY AND MATTHEW HAVE COME for a stay—like old times. They arrive in the bright early afternoon, and stand in the road, quiet: I guess they are remembering. The ivy is sparkling on the side of the wall, the sky has that blue it takes on only in October, a light breeze is blowing, one of the thirty-four Provençal winds that is neither the mistral nor the sirocco, and the weather is perfect for a walk on the Ventoux. Or anywhere else. Nicolas de Staël's small painting *Road in the Vaucluse* has just the feeling of this endless possibility: so unlocalized, such low-key colors, so open to wherever you might like to go, over that hill.

I have just been to swim in the lake, latish, so I had it all to myself. I could hear my breathing regular in the water and the swish of my left arm pulling out of the water, evenly. I drove home in my old 2CV with some Scarlatti playing, and felt at peace. Just now, I have placed my espadrilles, wet from my putting them on too hastily afterward, upon the low tile roof upstairs, high enough for the neighbor's dog not to find them. I put on my other pair and remind my children, now grown-up, where they can find some, in the little trunk where I have always kept bathing suits, sweaters, and extra espadrilles of all sizes. They find their old ones, Hilary's lavender and Matthew's blue pair, and look decidedly happier so shod. Hilary has gone off to check on the whereabouts of her favorite insects. She has always had a special relationship with the animal world.

To celebrate Matthew's birthday in August, we had always gone up the Ventoux. Now we go up, out of season, Matthew at the wheel. It is slow going in our beloved dilapidated 2CV. We clamber around, freezing at the top despite all the sweaters we have piled on. Then, exhausted and happy, we climb back in the car and make our way down to the halfway stop at the plateau of Groseaux—Great Waters—where a little stream runs through rocks and there are picnic tables and a tiny stone chapel right after. I have brought an afternoon *goûter* for us: bitter chocolate and faintly sweet Lu biscuits, with a bottle of chilled Beaumes de Venise—our favorite, from the Domaine d'Urban, far up the hill where our Deux Chevaux could barely make it. Why ever go down the mountain we wonder.

Mainly because of the cabanon. Because of the melons on the boot scraper above the basil plants against the ochre wall with its ivy; the apricots in a glazed bowl inside on the yellow oilcloth, next to the single lemon, and the tomatoes, ripe in the earthenware dish. Because this is the place to be together. Or alone. We lay out on the steep stone steps our supper of sausage, bread, cheese, grapes, and wine, and put a candle on the table.

We have time. Later, we will stretch out some sleeping bags and blankets upon the ground upstairs under the stars, bluish white. Matthew has brought with him a cassette of Mahler's *Das Lied von der Erde,* and the sound of Kathleen Ferrier singing "The Song of the Earth" will stretch all the way to the cherry trees at the other end of the field.

In the winter, there will be hearty soups, and the rain will fall on the tile roof. The wood remaining in the field from the dead cherry tree will be chopped to burn: the chill is intense. Truffles, some found at the foot of our own cherry trees by the truffle dogs—first suckled with the taste of truffles rubbed on the mother dog's teats—will be sold in the markets, the men standing around on corners, nonchalant with their small brown bags to gather them in. Hail will come, and frost, and the snow will sit on the Ventoux. The vines will climb higher up the stone walls. The cabanon, if I can trust its beams and its endurance, will hold firm in the seasons to come. Whoever comes here will know this.

TIDES

After so much had happened, after my divorce—a sort of unhinging until finally a sort of rehinging—I would often go home to visit Mother and Peg in Oleander, in a smaller house when we had sold the one we grew up in, after Father died. Once, in the early fall when it was neither hot nor chilly, Mother took me completely by surprise. She asked me, so abruptly that I was startled by the invitation, if I would like to go swimming with her in the sound. We were nowhere near Wrightsville Beach, where we had had no place for years, and went only sometimes on a summer day to swim, using the Yacht Club to change clothes—I remember the smell of wet wood there, the feeling of the boardwalk burning under our feet. Then the building closed for the season.

It had just now begun to rain, and the twilight was already dimming—a very odd moment to choose. But Mother might have looked in the paper to see when it was high tide in the sound, and decided accordingly on her invitation. Or more probably it was her native intuition, by which she decided so much—and which I inherited, for bad and good. Mother was then well over seventy and not at all strong. We hadn't been swimming together for quite a few years.

Trying not to appear in the slightest surprised, "Of course," I answered, "of course." I didn't let on how perplexed I was, I just put on my bathing suit under my jeans and followed her to the car. We both rolled down the windows to catch the breeze, as we always had.

We drove down to the beach in silence, and left our towels on the public pier, since ours was someone else's now, and entered the water rather gingerly under the pelting rain.

The rain is making diagonal streaks on the silver water. No one in sight anywhere. We swim through the choppy water a little way out. It isn't cold like the air. Side by side, we keep up the same slow rhythm in the water as it changes from silver to greyish black. Once we exchange a smile. Now we can barely see each other. We don't go far out. We don't have to.

Then we turned around, climbed back up on the pier shivering, wrapped our towels around us, and went home in the growing darkness. Driving back, we didn't say anything. But we had swum together, when the night was coming on.

When Mother became ill, Peg came home from South Carolina, where she had been presenting television programs about teaching, as she had earlier in New York. Mother never felt alone, for Peg was there with her. When Mother died, Nunny wasn't there anymore to talk with us. So we just did the best we could. I can still see Mother straining, her eyes fixed on some distant spot and her arms reaching forward, rocking back and forth in her bed the way Father had on the beach porch, in a rhythm that did not stop, as she went her way to meet her Maker. She had been hoping to go for some time, and I expect he was glad to have her at last.

She had decided shortly before the end, with Peg, to be buried in Saint James's churchyard among the plants and flowers—a new kind of graveyard, in a sense about living instead of dying. So she would never lie by her husband in the Oakdale cemetery plot where we had seen him lowered into the grave under the flag, with taps playing, finally at peace. In that cemetery where Grandmother lay by the side of her husband, and where, young and less young, we had looked every Easter at the grave of little Charlie and his lamb, Mother's first stone will continue to read simply:

Margaret Devereux Lippitt Rorison
1900–

because she is not buried there. We decided never to take that inscription in the graveyard away. I find this odd, outdated, chiseled, and unfinalized statement something of a miracle. Mother deserves, as I see it, to have her future open somewhere.

At Mother's funeral, I came down alone, for Peter and I had been divorced long before. We had come down together for Father's funeral, when he was buried in the cemetery, and that had been a very different occasion: we had been close. This time, before going to the church, Peg and I sent the now grown-up children to look at those vines above the creek. It was as if they had always known where they hung.

Peg had planned the service, with all the hymns Mother loved, that her father had loved before her:

> Rock of ages, cleft for me,
> Let me *hide* myself in *thee,*

with an accent on the upslide: "let me hide" and on the end, "in thee." It wasn't that we believed anything very firmly, but that we knew how deeply she had.

We stood side by side in the church, Peg and I, next to the children. We sang Mother's favorite of all hymns. Matthew's voice was deeper than I remembered, and he took my hand:

Now the day is o—ver
Night is draw—ing ni—gh
Shadows of the eve—ning
Steal across the sk—y.

After the service, we stood side by side in the church garden. On Mother's remains in the garden, we each threw a handful of dirt.

Then we all went home—now Peg's, for she had shared it with Mother—without saying much. There wasn't a lot to say. Nobody talked about forgetting or forgiving or guilt or anything, we just went home as if we still lived there and sat in the pantry close together.

It stands out clearly for me now. Things aren't so tangled up any more.

Yes, we sat in the pantry, crowding together on the little white benches. Since Nunny wasn't there, I made custard for all of us, so we could have it smooth and hot from the oven, with lots of nutmeg grated over it. It was good.

BACK TO THE BOATHOUSE

That smell of plaster of paris in my grandmother's dark-shingled mountain studio comes rushing in again with the sight of the morning glories pressing blue against the walls. An old ring made for her in Venice has replaced my wedding ring—I won't be taking that one off. The light in her eyes may reach over to me this morning, as if, no longer here, she could teach me all the same. Now is when I want to learn. Her energy is there somewhere, ready to be passed on. To me, and maybe from me.

It can wait: no rush. I can learn patience.

Yesterday I went out to Southhampton, one of the places Grandmother studied and painted, when she could get away. I rented a pink bike, its wire basket hanging sideways, and pushed out to the sea along the deserted roads. She would have done that, as I imagine her, in her long skirt.

> *When I go out on my bike in the summer heat, past the museum, over to the park, the raised bumps in the hot asphalt almost upset my old Raleigh, before I reach the peace and the green of the park. I take my coffee in the hot cup brimming over at the edges to the table in front of the open window by the lake. At the boathouse, things always seem hopeful.*

I remember, one fall day, returning to the boathouse with the children, grown-ups now. That night Hilary and I were going, with Hilary's husband, Jonathan, to hear Matthew's group, performing very late in the Mercury Lounge. I knew they would play his song that I found so sad and right, "80 Windows," with a line about his companion liking the window across the way:

> You said you like the one
> With the father who always eats with his son . . .

And then Matthew would sing, about himself:

> I like the rows of lights because they keep me calm,

before the refrain:

> The moon is closer to the sun
> Than I am to anyone . . .

It was a mild day for October, slightly fogged over yet with a sheen over everything. "It's all different!" said Hilary, and then suggested we might take a rowboat on the lake. "Of course," Matthew and I said both at once. Jonathan laughed that wonderful laugh.

It is such a clear memory—we took three coffees and an orange juice and the rowboat ticket, and ran, all four of us, to the dock, Matthew's guitar banging against his side. In the middle of the lake, Matthew began to play, "I want to know what it's like," he sang, "on the inside of love." We grinned at each other and lifted our paper cups to toast the lake and our city. "What about going home now?" asked Hilary. "This is home too," said Matthew.

This telling was once to be about growing up in the South. About some tanglings up and some clearing, and then about a boathouse farther north, another kind of home. It's a story and yet it's true, as far as I can see it. It's funny how it matters where you start being you. I started there, in the southern Tidewater. Now I live somewhere else, but not only. Grandmother knew home was wherever you were and decided to be and dwell. You are wherever you can speak from. I think I've found the right address.

> Discovery does not imply that the place is new, only that we are.
> —Eudora Welty, "Place in Fiction"